The Canary Islander

Barrie Mahoney worked as a teacher and head teacher in the south west of England, and then became a school inspector in England and Wales. A new life and career as a newspaper reporter in Spain's Costa Blanca led to him launching and editing an English language newspaper in the Canary Islands. Barrie's books include novels in 'The Prior's Hill Chronicles' series, as well as books in the 'Letters from the Atlantic' series, which give an amusing and reflective view of life abroad.

Barrie writes regular columns for newspapers and magazines in Spain, Portugal, Ireland, Australia, South Africa, Canada, UK and the USA. He also designs mobile apps and websites to promote life in the Canary Islands, and is often asked to contribute to radio programmes.

Visit the author's websites:

www.barriemahoney.com
www.thecanaryislander.com

Other books by Barrie Mahoney

Journeys & Jigsaws (The Canary Islander Publishing) 2013
ISBN: 978 184386 646 6 (Paperback and eBook)

Threads and Threats (The Canary Islander Publishing) 2013
ISBN: 978 184386 645 9 (Paperback and eBook)

Letters from the Atlantic (The Canary Islander Publishing) 2013
ISBN: 978-0992767136 (Paperback and eBook)

Living the Dream (The Canary Islander Publishing) 2011
ISBN: 978 145076 704 0 (Paperback and eBook)

Message in a Bottle (The Canary Islander Publishing) 2012
ISBN: 978-1480031005 (Paperback and eBook)

Escape to the Sun (The Canary Islander Publishing) 2012
ISBN: 978-0957544444 (Paperback and eBook)

Voices from Spain & the Canary Islands

Barrie Mahoney

The Canary Islander Publishing

The
Canary
Islander

ISBN 978-1068284922
www.barriemahoney.com

First Published 2014
Second Edition 2025

The Canary Islander Publishing

Acknowledgements

I would like to thank all those people that I have met on my journey to where I am now.

To supportive friends who helped me to overcome the many problems and frustrations that I faced and taught me much about learning to adapt to a new culture. Also, to friends in the UK, or scattered around the world, who have kept in touch despite being so far away.

To the people that I met whilst working as a newspaper reporter and editor in Spain and the Canary Islands, and for the privilege of sharing their successes and challenges in life.

Disclaimer

This is a book about real people, real places and real events, but names of people and companies have been changed to avoid any embarrassment.

The
Canary
Islander

DEDICATION

This book is dedicated to those who dream of a new life, new experiences, new cultures, new opportunities to experience, taste and smell the excitement of a place that is of their own choosing and not merely based upon an accident of birth.

The
Canary
Islander

Contents

Preface

Preface

My weekly blog 'Twitters from the Atlantic' was initially intended as a brief follow up to my novel 'Letters from the Atlantic', which were published in a local newspaper. This weekly series has since appeared in magazines, newspapers and blogs in many countries across the world, and I have been surprised and heartened by the enthusiastic response that I have received, as well as from those considering 'living their dream' in a country of their own choosing.

After the first series of 'Twitters from the Atlantic' was published, I began to receive requests from many readers who, for various reasons, had missed a specific article, asking if I could get a back copy of the newspaper or magazine for them. Eventually, it was suggested that I should publish the entire series of blogs for the year in one volume. That was ten years ago! I am now pleased to be able to publish the latest in the series - this time called 'Voices from Spain & the Canary Islands'.

I chose this title because many of the incidents that are raised in the book arose from emails, letters and conversations from people in a number of countries, as well as from my own experiences. We all have our individual tales to tell, and I am always impressed by the enthusiasm and (mostly!) good humour that demonstrated when dealing with both challenges and amusing incidents in their new lives. This book is intended to be an echo of those voices, which I hope will prove to be of both help and inspiration to others.

Looking at some of the early 'Twitters from the Atlantic', I am reminded of the huge enthusiasm that affects us all when we embark upon our new adventure. A new country, new customs and traditions, as well as often a new language, all add to the thrill of escaping from the country of our birth. However, as time and experience take over, most of us must deal with new challenges in life, which we may not have originally envisaged.

This book attempts to deal with some of the challenges faced following the World recession, which has left many without jobs, failed relationships and repossessed homes. For many, it has not been a wonderful experience, but I am a firm believer that, over time, such difficulties make us stronger if approached in a positive and realistic manner. I know of many who appear to have 'failed', but have 'bounced back' stronger and more resilient to the challenges that life throws at us all from time to time.

Unusually, in this book, I have tried to deal with other, more serious, issues that many have asked me to write about. Often taboo subjects, such as dealing with serious illness, death and wills have been raised in 'Voices'. Despite my original anxiety, it is a relief to see that pages dealing with 'Death' and 'Wills' on my website have received the most number of hits from readers this year, so I guess these articles have served a useful purpose for some; I hope so.

Life for people from any country, be it for reasons of work, retirement, or just following a spirit of adventure, is not always as easy as it may sound. A new life in the sun is often frustrated by having to deal with personal and family crises, health issues, language difficulties, confusing bureaucracy and cultural differences. This is all the stuff of adventures, which is part of the deal that we signed up for. The wise and seasoned traveller eventually learns to accept and cope with a range of issues, which is part of our rich kaleidoscope of experiences. Personally, I wouldn't have it any other way.

Voices

Voices

So what do you think about democracy and your right to vote? Sorry, but I can see you yawning already, but that cross in the box is important and many have struggled for years, and continue to give their lives, for the right to put a cross on the ballot paper every four or five years.

I was chatting to George the other day. Regular 'Twitter' readers will be familiar with my friend, George. Without doubt, he is the most boring and irritating friend that I know; he finds fault with everything and everyone. However, I continue to have dinner with him from time to time, as I find that he stimulates my argumentative juices and his distorted view of the world can be refreshing, and occasionally illuminating. We were on the subject of voting in the forthcoming European elections.

"I don't bother to vote any more," George announced as he was shoving a large piece of steak into his mouth. "There's no point, and it never makes any difference."

I sighed. I toyed with the vegetarian lasagne on my plate, determined not to let George rile me so early in the evening. He was not a bad man, but he really was not an asset to the community, and would be far better moving back to Preston, where he could get all the Brit sausages, pork pies and bacon that he loved so much.

"Don't you think it is your democratic duty, George? After all, the right to vote has cost many people their lives and much suffering in the past. You have only to think of Emily Pankhurst..."

My earnest words fell on deaf ears and I let George continue with his anti-democratic protestations. I was wasting my breath. My mind wandered to a recent news report about a 93-year-old British man, Harry Schindler, who is living in Italy. He recently took the British Government to court for not allowing him to vote in British elections, even though he has been living in Italy for the last 30 years. He has been battling in the courts for the right to have his vote restored for the last 12 years.

I do not share Harry's views. Personally, I could not get out of the UK quick enough to start my new life in Spain, and continuing to vote in UK elections was the last thing on my mind at the time. I did, however, exercise my right to vote in both local and General Elections in the UK for about four years after I had left. Even though all are currently entitled to vote for 15 years after they have left the UK, I felt that I had no right to vote after I had left the country. Over time, I have become increasingly unaware of many British issues, and I have to confess that when I do return occasionally to the UK, I feel like a visitor returning to a foreign country.

I know that many will disagree with me. Certainly, many intend to return to the UK in time, whilst others will comment that British Government policy has a direct impact upon their family, pensions and finances, even though they are no longer living in the country, and therefore they have a right to vote. I respect their views, but would much prefer that I have full voting rights in my adopted country, Spain and the Canary Islands.

As it stands, I am entitled to vote in the European elections, as well as municipal elections in the Canary Islands. However, I have no right to vote in Spanish national or in the regional Canarian Government elections, as I am not a Spanish citizen. However, my home is in the Canary Islands, and I pay my share of local and national Spanish taxes, so being deprived of a vote seems just a little unreasonable, particularly after living in Spain for a lengthy period of time.

Back to the Harry Schinder story. The courts threw out Harry's claim that was aimed to change a British law that says that those that leave the UK can no longer vote in the country after living abroad for more than fifteen years. Schindler has not taken out Italian citizenship, which means that he too cannot participate in the country's elections. Harry is determined to fight on and intends to take the matter to the European Court of Human Rights, because he believes that British law breaches the Universal Declaration of Human Rights, which states everyone has the right to participate in the government of their country.

To me, this is precisely the point. I really would like the opportunity to vote in the government of the country where I live, work and pay taxes, but do not share Harry's wish of being able to vote in the elections of a country that I am no longer part of.

Does it matter? Well, without labouring the point too heavily, I believe that it does. Most contribute greatly to the local economy, as well as the society that they have become part of. Surely an appropriate gesture would be recognition that, after a period of time, we can use our democratic voices in our adopted countries.

"Yes, George. I know that that Farage fellow enjoys a drink and a smoke, but personally, I really would rather not have dinner with him."

At this point, I remembered my mother's wise words of never to talk about religion, politics, sex or vegetarianism at the dinner table.

"How about a nice dessert, George?"

Feuding

Recent emails from correspondents in France and Portugal, as well as Spain, have made me question how friendly people really are towards each other?

Personally, and very fortunately, I have experienced nothing but help and support from others during my time living and working in Spain and the Canary Islands. Our British and Irish friends were lifesavers to us during those early months when we were living in the Costa Blanca, and who have remained some of our closest and dearest friends. From being given a bed for a few nights by our new and very generous neighbours, when we discovered that we had no water or electricity in our new home, to Christmas dinners kindly delivered by other neighbours when I had a particularly bad case of flu; I have very little to complain about.

However, not everything in the garden is quite as rosy. I am well aware of the worries and concerns that many have when; for example, planning a dinner party or having friends around for the evening. Considerations such as "Who has fallen out with whom?", "Who is not speaking to whom?" and "Who has recently slept with whom and does his /her partner know?" are all important considerations for the proficient hostess to ponder over when preparing her paella. Such considerations can override such usual considerations, such as "Is she still vegetarian?" and "He is on a celeriac diet, what the hell can I give him to eat?" pale into blissful insignificance. Of course, such sensitivities have to be taken account of in our home countries too, but they are much more acute within a small community and, particularly, within a small island community.

Acute hostilities do exist between individuals and groups. The "we are all in it together" is fine for a time, but when one person appears to be increasing in social standing, doing better than his peers, gaining preferential employment opportunities, or has the audacity to buy a new car or install a Jacuzzi, then all hell can break loose. There are few things worse than jealousy.

There tend to be enclaves of particular nationalities in all popular areas, with the British and Irish sticking together, the Germans, the Norwegians and French all claiming their own particular 'areas', and often complete with their own schools, churches and even hospitals. Unhealthy as this may seem, it is understandable, because it gives a degree of protection in language, culture and behaviour that acts as a buffer against a sometimes hostile world, which is usually based upon a lack of understanding of local culture, laws and language.

There is also the 'Pecking Order' to consider. This can be a vicious beast in disguise, which one has to watch for. Many are usually immediately interrogated upon arrival by their peers, such as to where you come from, the number of years that you have spent in your 'new' country, whether or not you speak the language and, most importantly, what you do or what have you done for employment in your home country? This final question is, of course, the main indicator as to your placing in the social order of your new group of 'friends'. It is fine if you are a pensioner, but watch out if you say that you are unemployed. Top of the heap, of course, are those who speak the language, have knowledge of local culture, laws and traditions, those who are sleeping with a native, closely followed by those who had prestigious jobs in their home country, and whether or not you are perceived to "have money".

Of course, those who do not speak the language are forced to socialise together, whether or not they like it and it is those who are the most vulnerable when 'fallings out' and arguments take place. I have heard horrific accounts from several people whose main reason for returning 'home' was that they found their neighbours to be quite unbearable, and they were lonely because of lack of friends speaking in their own tongue.

Feuds can be avoided; for example, I quickly discovered, and particularly as a newspaper reporter, not to take sides on particular issues, such as animal welfare and, of course, local politics. Believe me, for all their good intentions, there is nothing worse than a group of animal welfare supporters in dispute with another group of animal welfare supporters; it is a bomb just waiting to explode. Despite the well-meaning intentions of both sides, both groups seem totally incapable of seeing the merits and good intentions of another.

My best advice for those planning to move abroad is, above all, learn the language before you arrive and, if possible, develop interests so that you can take part in local activities that involve the local population. In doing this, you will widen your involvement with the local community that you have opted to live amongst and develop a wider circle of friends, and rely less upon the local population. Mind you, there is still nothing quite like a few drinks and a good gossip with someone who speaks the same language and shares the same sense of humour.

Unhealthy

I have just returned from a wonderful two weeks in the UK. As usual, it was good to meet up with family and friends once again, as well as doing a little shopping in some of our favourite stores to buy a few of those special treats that most crave for. However, I also managed to pick up an unpleasant virus that meant I had to spend two days in bed in a hotel bedroom. It was all so frustrating.

I know exactly how it happened. The young man sitting in the seat in front of us on the crowded train from Gatwick Airport into London was coughing and spluttering. It was when he received a phone call from his mum and he informed her that he was on his way to the hospital that alarm bells rang. Yes, I know exactly where this particular bug came from.

As soon as I arrived home I made an appointment to see my doctor. We have a wonderful, yet small, health centre in our village. It is nearly always possible to make an appointment to see a doctor the following day, and appointments are efficiently made on the Internet. After examination I was diagnosed with a chest infection, given antibiotics, and plugged into a nebuliser that helped my breathing.

It is rare that I am ill, and I am not aware of any underlying health conditions. However, my doctor made the point that a rapid drop in temperature may have contributed to the problem. After all, it had been 36 degrees on the day that we had left Gran Canaria and ten degrees when we arrived in London. I had always assumed that wearing thermals, wrapping up well and wearing gloves and a hat would be all that is needed to deal with the colder climate, but apparently it is not.

A small-scale investigation of friends who have previously lived in Southern Spain, Portugal, France and the Canary Islands revealed that many now suffer from respiratory conditions, which began after their return to the UK, even though they were perfectly healthy when they lived in a warmer climate. One couple revealed to me that their UK doctor had warned them that the body takes a long time to adjust from a warm climate to a much cooler one, and that with some people the adjustment may never take place, particularly in older people. A cheery thought.

This is an area that I have not considered before, and I suspect very few people have either. Maybe this is something that intending travellers should consider when dreaming of a life in warmer climates upon retirement? If it is their intention to return to the UK at a later time, the adjustment may be difficult and cause additional health problems. I also suspect that little research has been carried out in this area. Maybe it is an ideal subject for a PhD thesis for a medical student?

Meanwhile, I am relieved to be home again and as soon as I get these pills and potions out of the way, I can resume my life in the sun.

Space

Well, its that time of the year again, and after all the goodwill has evaporated, the tinsel packed away for another year, the new diet started and you have considered suicide after receiving your credit card statement, you may be planning a holiday to get over it all. How about a holiday in the sun? I can recommend an ideal place, and that is the island of Gran Canaria.

No, just for once, I am not talking about a leisurely sunshine break on one of our wonderful beaches, enjoying incredible nightlife and mountain scenery that is little short of spectacular. Instead, how about being shot up one hundred kilometres into space for a rather lovely view of the Earth, or the blue planet as the travel brochures will soon be calling it?

As surprising as it might be, Gran Canaria, has been selected as the place to shoot three satellites into space over the next few years, together with an orbiting spaceship for passengers, and offering supersonic commercial flights between continents that will reach five times the speed of sound. The new Spaceport is to be built at the existing and newly refurbished airport in Gran Canaria, which folk often forget is the third largest in Spain.

The small spaceship, known as SOAR, will indeed be cosy, offering accommodation for six passengers and two pilots, but I was sad to see that there will be no air flight attendants on board. How I will miss those safety demonstrations, in flight meals and sales of duty free, but I guess they will discover another way to get passengers to part with more cash. How about optional high quality oxygen for sale? After recent experiences with my fridge, cooker and dishwasher, of which country and make will remain anonymous, I was delighted to discover that it is the Swiss who will be designing and building the spacecraft. After all, even after a few hundred years, they still make such reliable watches, and I am sure that their time keeping and reliability will be impeccable.

This major new project will provide a tremendous boost to the economy of the island, with 60 million euros being invested in the project, together with the creation of new highly skilled jobs. However, given the island's desperate attempts to block the major oil-drilling project off the eastern Canary Islands, which is supposed to create all manner of environmental disasters, and its preferences for 'green' energy and environmentally friendly policies, I fail to see how this is compatible with a major carbon producing activity such as launching spacecraft. No doubt the politicians will have an answer for me shortly.

I was also initially pleased and later dismayed to learn that the island has been selected because of its closeness to West Africa and Europe, as well as providing easy access to the Atlantic Ocean. Well, I cannot argue with the logic of that one, but the statement goes on to say that it is ideal for the launch of satellites, because there are no major centres of population below. Hmm, well, as myself and many other happen to live quite close to the airport, I am not quite so sure that they have selected the right location.

—

Of course, Richard Branson has already taken the first leap into space tourism. Not being content with offering banking and mobile phone services, he has created Virgin Galactic, which is due to launch from New Mexico in the US next year. There is already a waiting list of 500 people willing to pay around 150,000 euros for a flight, but Gran Canaria is just so more convenient for us Europeans.

There we have it, Gran Canaria is clearly the only place to travel to for a vacation, whether it be on the beach or in space. All in all, I am rather excited about the whole idea and will be busily trying to find the odd 3000 euros, which will be the price of a ticket, tucked in the back of the sofa. It sounds like a great idea for a future holiday, but just as long as there are no tour reps on board trying to flog overpriced excursions, or time-share touts trying to sell me a holiday home on the Moon, even with imported white sand, I will be happy.

You are so lucky! A reality check

I was recently asked to speak at a meeting. It was one of those question-and-answer forums, which provided the opportunity for established residents to bare their souls about things that they both liked and disliked in their new lives, as well as providing an opportunity for the newly arrived to learn something from the experiences of others.

I was struck by a comment from one lady who made the point that she both hated, as well as felt guilty, whenever her friends and family in the UK, made the comment that, "You are just so lucky…" Judging from the nods and murmurs of approval from others around her, she had made a point that many others also recognised. I certainly do, and it is a comment that also irritates me. In my experience, we create our own good fortune in life, and I can think of very few who have not worked hard to create a new life for themselves in another country.

The thoughts of moving to another country in the sunshine, when peering out of the window to endless rain and fog and surrounded by floods, is understandably appealing. However, many 'would be' residents forget the downsides of not being in a country that speaks the same language, the significant differences in customs and traditions, as well as dealing with legal and financial systems that may seem unnecessarily complicated to those who are newly arrived. Many are involved for years in fighting legal and property disputes with their neighbours, town halls or property developers. Of course, many problems stem from not understanding the language and culture, as well as the legal traditions of their new country, and being swept along by the idea of starting a new life in the sun.

When I worked as a reporter in the Costa Blanca, my colleagues and I often commented in despair that when Brits left the UK, many left their brains at home. So many seemed to get themselves into dangerous legal and financial situations that they would not have considered in their home country. Maybe it is the effects of the heady combination of too much sunshine, as well as gin and tonics that are at the root of the problem. However, back to the meeting…

Homesickness and missing family and friends, British food and British television were all some of the predicable responses to questions asked about what they miss most. Interestingly, those who seemed to have settled best of all in their adopted country were those that had tried to learn the language, those who worked or were involved in local community or charity work, as well as those who had a sensitivity and interest in the local culture and traditions.

It was very easy to spot those who were less successful when they began most sentences with "When we lived in Preston, we used to…" or "Why don't the Spanish do it in the same way we used to in the UK?" Indeed, the first rule of being a successful traveller is, as tempting as it might be, to forget comparisons with your home country. Accept things as they are and try to work with them, rather than to fight against them.

Are we lucky? One thing became very clear from this meeting; nothing is handed over on a plate; it is not luck, but courage that makes the difference. In short, you need guts to be a successful traveller.

Pickled Onions and Red Squirrels

"Woman chokes to death on pickled onion", screamed the headlines of the local newspaper. Another headline, further down the page, caught my eye - "Temperatures to hit 80 degrees - hotter than the Canary Islands". Some things never change; I remembered the local newspaper as always being very good on headlines, but rather weaker on actual news. Still, I did feel sorry for the pickled onion lady and her family, as well as reflecting on whether she would have survived if it had been a pickled egg.

I had just returned for a rare, but brief visit to my UK home town of Bournemouth for a book event. It's not that I don't like the UK; on the contrary I am still very fond of the country, it's just that I am much happier living in the Canary Islands. I hoped that I had brought enough warm clothing with me. I needn't have worried; the weather was perfect and allowed me to indulge in visits to places that I loved.

My first visit was to Brownsea Island, in Poole Harbour, during the next glorious sunny day. I had fallen in love with this special place as a child, and continued to visit the island each year for many years during my days as a teacher, with parties of chattering school children. We were always intent upon seeing a red squirrel, but in those days, no self respecting red squirrel would dream of making itself known to 60 children under the age of eleven, clutching a worksheet and asking when they could stop for a drink or the toilet during our walk across the island. This time, as I sat in the tearoom indulging in a Dorset cream tea, I actually spotted two baby red squirrels playing together on the lawn in front of me. It was a sight that I had waited to see for many years.

As I sat watching the scene in front of me unfold, I began to reflect upon another island - the island that has been my home for the last ten years or so, Gran Canaria, one of the seven main Canary Islands. Even after a day or two, I had already begun to long for home as I was once again feeling that the UK had become a 'foreign country' to me. The currency was unfamiliar, I was now driving on the 'wrong side of the road', and the town seemed busier and more frenetic than I previously remembered. Some of my favourite shops had closed, there were new roads, and all the shop assistants seemed to be from another country. Traditional, grubby buses that had once ploughed infrequently through the town's streets had disappeared, replaced by smart, clean, colourful buses, with an unfamiliar name, which appeared every few minutes or so.

All too soon my brief visit to the UK was concluded, and I bought a selection of the usual treats that we cannot get at home. Sadly, I was flying with my least favourite airline; I had little choice at the time of booking, but hoped that their customer service had improved since the previous occasion. Sadly, I was wrong, and I was once again trapped in a cylinder full of people who had already drunk far too much alcohol before they boarded. Vodka and coke were spilt on seats with generous abandon, with cabin crew intent upon pouring yet more liquor down the throats of their young passengers. At least the cabin crew did not indulge in a novel game of "Throw and Catch the Toilet Roll" which had so entertained the staff, as well as infuriating passengers, on the flight to Tenerife the previous week.

I settled to listen to a selection of soothing songs on my phone; I was grateful that the ear pods cut out most of the shrieking cacophony of noise from the group sitting behind me. Foolishly, I bought a sandwich from the trolley, but the steward claimed that he had no change. I handed over a note and was promised that the change "would be brought to me shortly". I never did receive the change, despite mentioning it towards the end of the flight. I did not really expect to receive it, since the same thing had happened to me on two previous flights with this airline. I began to ponder on how much staff salaries were boosted by this little scam. I did not complain; I was just grateful to be reaching home and getting out of this tube of insanity at the earliest opportunity.

Finally, we landed. The pilot played its usual trumpet salvo to announce that we had landed, as if it was some kind of celebration that he had actually managed to hit the tarmac in the right place. I escaped as soon as I could, vowing as usual, never to travel with this airline of nightmares ever again.

Overall, it had been a good visit, but once again confirmed to me that the UK was no longer home. I had no longings and no regrets, but was just so pleased to be at home once again on our island in the sun.

Terrorist

Life is always full of surprises in Spain and the Canary Islands; nothing is ever quite what it seems, and this week has been no exception. I received a letter from the bank that I have been with since we moved to Spain demanding information. Parts of the letter were written in red ink as well as block capitals, which I assumed was meant to stress those parts that I should fret about most.

This letter was all part of a curt communication pointing out that under "Law 10/2010 of 28 April on the Prevention of Money Laundering and the Funding of Terrorism", the bank had an obligation to check my identity and professional activity. The letter then went on to say that if I did not comply with their demands, my account would be "restricted", meaning that I could not use their Internet banking and other services. Fortunately, there is no capital punishment in Spain at the moment; otherwise I am sure that they would have threatened that as well.

The letter also demanded payslips, social security employment records (vida laboral), my annual VAT return for the last quarter, or proof of having paid the last social security self-employed contribution. I am not registered, nor do I pay VAT, my accountant deals with social security contributions and I have not seen a vida laboral for at least five years.

Now I am all for countering terrorism and money laundering, but I doubt many offenders would use my local branch. This delightful letter was from a bank that I have used and trusted since I first set foot in

Spain, and the branch knows me well. Clearly, this was another of the games that we have to play in Spain from time to time, which I am well used to. It can be endless fun, if viewed from the right angle, but it is no good arguing with the system or getting angry. One merely has to appear humble and confused, smile a lot, claim insanity or not understanding the language. Above all, one has to swamp the system with paperwork, and lots of it.

I learned many years ago that Spanish bureaucracy loves nothing more than paper. One has only to wave a sheet of A4 across the eyes of a Spanish bureaucrat or bank official, and watch their facial expression glaze over, and turn into one of immense and immediate greed. These officials are well trained and can smell a document in your possession from a hundred paces. They snatch the document from you and, if you are fortunate, hurry off to the nearest photocopier to produce at least three copies, returning the original. If one is naive or unfortunate, they will grab the original and it is never seen again. This is very dangerous and inconvenient, and I learned many years ago NEVER to produce an original document for any bank or government official. The second thing that all Spanish officials have is a love affair with the fax machine, and it is more than likely that any document that you surrender will end up in one.

Back to the letter from my bank. I spent most of the day producing a box file of photocopies of all the documents that I thought would interest them. In view of their huge appetite for paperwork of any description, I have also learned never to volunteer anything, but to let it be requested, and certainly not to hand over a complete box file voluntarily.

I placed all the documents in a carrier bag with my shopping. When I arrived at the bank, I met a charming young bank clerk, who seemed anxious to attend to my every need and, in particular, get me to sign up for a loan that I didn't need. I handed over the offending letter; he smiled and nodded knowingly, and asked for my residency document and passport. He made a joke about the possibility of me being a terrorist, to which I smiled through gritted teeth. The young bank clerk then proceeded to photocopy my passport and residency certificate, which they have done many times before over the years. No other questions were asked and no other documents were requested. For once, I was in and out of the bank in five minutes. Now what was that all about?

There's Wind Up My Barranco

Living in the Canary Islands, I quickly learned that most people living in Northern European countries have little time for our occasional complaints about the weather. After all, as an Ancient Greek once declared, we live in the "Fortunate Islands"; the weather is as near perfect as we can get in Europe, and survey after survey has proven that these islands are the healthiest places in the World to live.

Does this mean that we never complain about the weather? Sadly not; after all, due to our early conditioning as Brits, others, as well as myself still complain about the weather from time to time. It is part of who we are, and an important part of our collective national psyche. It may be complaints about the weather being too hot, which it often is in August, too windy in July and even too wet - albeit for about three days in February.

We live quite close to what is often billed as "The Windiest Place on Earth". That place is the village of Pozo Izquierdo, home of the World Windsurfing Championships, and the place to go to watch spectacular waves and to enjoy the surf. Well, it would have to be windy there, wouldn't it? After all, little or no wind would make for a very sad or non-existent World Windsurfing Competition. However, the downside is that sometimes the winds in the area are so strong that they carry sand, soil, dust and goodness knows what else to towns and villages across a large part of the island.

Occasionally, the wind is too strong to even take Bella, our dog, for more than just a very short walk on the open land outside our village, and I have often considered buying her some goggles in order to cope with the sand and dust, as it bites into our eyes as we walk. It is often challenging to face and walk against these strong winds, and I have occasionally seen children and small adults swept off their feet, as well as the occasional vehicle overturned on our busy motorway.

This year has been exceptionally bad for strong winds, with sand and soil piled up against the sides of properties and the edges of roads after a particularly windy period. With the sand and dust, also comes a range of bacteria, which often results in breathing disorders and eye infections. Admittedly, it is only for a short period of the year, and is forgotten as quickly as it came.

Readers may well be asking why we chose to live in such a windy spot on the island, and living in windy areas is not for the faint hearted. However, recognising that there is no such thing as perfection in life, and after trying out several locations on the island over a few years, we came to the conclusion that we would much rather face the refreshing, albeit sometimes violent, winds on the east coast, rather than being cooked alive in the south of the island during July and August. High temperatures may be great for a holiday, but I am still very happy to exchange excessive temperatures for cooling breezes. As far as weather is concerned, we are very fortunate and have little to complain about. However, as a Brit, it is important to retain our national identity and complain about the weather from time to time.

Island Culture

The
Canary
Islander

The Music Bus

I have recently taken to travelling more frequently by bus on the island, particularly if I wish to visit our capital centre, Las Palmas de Gran Canaria. I dislike negotiating the ever changing one-way streets in the city, which we often forget is the seventh largest city in Spain, or trying to find a car park that is invariably full or horrendously expensive. I have also had my fair share of parking fines, as well as recently being 'ticked off' by a very kind, young policeman who met me heading the wrong way up a one-way street. In my defence, the direction of this one-way street had once again recently been changed, and no one had bothered to tell me about it. He was a very nice young man, and after I had explained that I was a confused Brit, he put his handcuffs back on his belt and sent me merrily on my way to my favourite department store. Nowadays, I have come to the conclusion that I would much prefer to negotiate the streets of central London; it would be so much easier.

Another reason that I like travelling by bus is that it is such a social occasion in Gran Canaria. One of my hobbies is people watching, and I can sit in a bar for hours observing human nature and imagining appropriate scenarios for them, which may appear in the novel that I happen to be writing at the time. The bus is a natural extension of this curious interest as, believe me, Canarian buses are filled with some of the most gregarious, happy and friendly people that you would ever wish to meet. These people do not need alcohol or drugs to have a good time; it just seems to come naturally to them.

Last week, my partner and I returned from Las Palmas after a shopping trip in the city. The bus service on the island is excellent, and the bus was already waiting to leave by the time that we got on board. The bus driver was a chirpy soul; I guess in his late thirties. I could tell at once that he was a man who actually liked people, which, if you think about it, is often a rare quality nowadays, particularly in any service industry. He had a cheeky banter with each passenger as they entered his domain, and we also received a few words of welcoming Spanish. He grinned at my feeble effort to make a small joke in Spanish, but I felt that he was appreciative of the effort that I had made.

It was just after we left the bus station that the fun, or should I say music, began. Fernando, as we all quickly discovered after his announcement, suddenly surprised us with a CD recording of a piano recital of music from musical shows, as well as other popular classics. This was not the usual sound of a badly tuned radio, broadcasting football, news or the latest chart busters, but a full concert performance, with the sound turned on full volume throughout the bus. Was it pure coincidence that we found ourselves listening to the merry tinkling of "I did it my way" as we passed the mortuary, I wondered?

On our one-hour journey home, we were regaled with music ranging from Abba, Phantom of the Opera to the Beatles. It was just after one of the Abba melodies, that there was a huge cheer and applause from the passengers, with many singing along loudly to the music. It was amusing to watch the faces of some of the young hoodies that appeared on board from time to time, and to watch their expressions when they suddenly realised that they were going to be forced to listen to "uncool" music for the full length of their journey. Some young rebels gathered together at the back of the bus, desperately trying to initiate a campaign to overcome the piano music with rap or the latest Canarian music from the feeble speakers of their mobile phones. Sadly, they would have needed a 70s 'ghetto blaster' to overcome Fernando's special musical treat for his passengers.

At one point, one of Fernando's colleagues got on the bus, which I assume was for a lift back to the bus depot. He too joined in with the merriment, but also added energetic hand actions and foot tapping. Our driver enthusiastically accompanied the music with improvised percussion, created by tapping the hollow part his ticket machine. At one point I thought they would be giving out YMCA hats to all the passengers, so that we could all join in.

We were actually rather sad to finally reach our destination. We left the bus still humming some of the tunes that we had been forced to listen to during our late afternoon of Fernando's musical entertainment. It may not have been our choice of music, but it certainly brought a smile to our faces, as well as the other passengers.

Was this a one off? Well, I am led to believe that Fernando has a special reputation for his music bus, which has become an institution on this particular bus route. Sadly, I cannot see it being popular on London Transport buses. I am sure that there are some health

and safety or licencing rules against it, but this is
Gran Canaria!

Kissing in the Canaries

I am often asked why I love the Canary Islands, and Gran Canaria, in particular, so much and what prompted us to make this small Atlantic island our home.

Well, I could move into lyrical mode about the wonderful climate, beautiful beaches, spectacular mountain scenery, the unhurried pace of life and the friendly unassuming nature of the locals... All this is true, but the main reason for moving here is none of these, although they are all part of the cocktail that led us to start our packing and head for the islands some years ago.

For me, it was and still is, the 'live and let live' attitude of the locals, and most of the visitors to this island, that made this a special place, and worthy to call 'home'. It has always been the case that most things are acceptable here, just as long as it doesn't hurt or interfere with anyone else.

I wonder just how many of our visitors attend the 'Welcome Meetings' that used to be the delight of many tour companies some years ago? A cheap glass of sangria was supposed to earn oodles of euros in commission for the tour reps, but sadly I never found their sales patter that convincing. I recall one tour representative begging us not to take the local bus to Puerto Mogan, because apparently the locals travel on the bus with baskets of live chickens on market days. A 20 euro coach excursion would apparently be much less pungent... All stuff and nonsense, of course, as we all know that the locals much prefer to travel with a goat.

I contrast these islands' attitudes to Austria, for instance, where the Viennese authorities have recently banned kissing on the train, alongside eating smelly food and talking too loudly. Well, I am not sure what the good people of Austria would think of travelling on a Canarian bus, but talking, and indeed kissing, quietly is certainly not on the agenda over here. I remain convinced that Spanish and Canarian children are born with a volume control that is permanently glued in the 'Exceedingly Loud' position. Most find it impossible to speak quietly, and why should they? After all, they have many interesting things to say. In any case, the mobile phone networks are not too good over here, and so it is essential to shout loudly at all times when making a telephone call.

If you should happen to venture to Austria for a holiday, do please be aware that you are now subject to an immediate fine of 50 euros should you happen to show your affection by kissing on the train. Husband, wife, boyfriend or girlfriend, concubine or simply a 'bit on the side'; it simply does not matter whether it is a quick peck on the cheek or a tongue job; you will still be relieved of a crisp 50 euro note by a very cross man in uniform.

How about a nice bag of chips on the way home, a slice of pizza or, the Canarian's favourite snack, a sticky donut? Sorry, but if in Austria it won't just be an immediate slap on the wrists and a fine of 50 euros, but you will be thrown off the train by a specially appointed 'jobsworth', locally known as sheriffs, and they have a badge to prove it.

Apparently, these draconian rules have been introduced as a result of complaints from the good citizens of Austria, as well from the results of a public survey. Mind you, they might have a point since a couple were recently discovered to be having sex on board a train; well, I guess it is more spacious than having sex in a Mini. In another highly disturbing case, one wealthy couple took their pet horse, Helga, on the train for a ride. I find this a very disturbing story, since it is common knowledge that most horses will only travel first class nowadays. Sadly, both cases were judged as being far too serious for the appointed 'jobsworth' to deal with, but became police matters and the culprits were thrown into prison. However, I am not too sure what happened to the horse, but maybe she is still partying in Vienna.

Well, I know it takes all sorts to make a world, but I for one will be cancelling my holiday in Austria next year. Personally, I am really looking forward to my next journey on a Canarian bus.

The Musical Onion Man

The sound of a flute playing a short piercing melody interrupted my writing this morning. I looked out of the window and spotted a tall, young man standing in his jeep playing a flute. In the back of the battered old vehicle were boxes of dried, plump onions. After a second or two of playing his cheerful tune, he would drive the vehicle a little further down the road, where he would stop, pick up his flute and repeat the melody. Sadly, he had chosen the wrong time of day, as most of our neighbours were out at work, but one elderly woman did buy a string of onions from him. I could hear laughter from the old woman in response to his cheeky banter, as his vehicle turned and swept out of sight.

This brief incident reminded me of a story that my mother told me long ago about Spanish onion sellers who used to travel from village to village in the UK selling strings of onions from their bicycles. The same onion sellers used to appear at about the same time each year, and village folk would look forward to their visits and often buy strings of onions from them. Spanish onions have, of course, a well-deserved reputation for being particularly delicious, as, it would seem, did many of the onion sellers.

I remember a story about one of my mother's teenage girl friends who, over a period of two or three years, received regular visits from a Spanish onion seller. By all accounts, he was a particularly handsome and rugged young man, who always had a friendly banter with all he met, whether or not they bought onions from him. He became particularly friendly with one pretty young woman, and it was quickly noticed by many in the village that her family was receiving rather more visits and a greater share of onions than most. It didn't take the village gossips long to work out that the young woman was receiving a great deal more than onions from this attractive young man.

Matters in the village became rather unpleasant and the young woman quickly became ostracised by those who thought that she was "behaving no better than she should". However, the story ended happily because, one day, the onion seller appeared for the final time and whisked the young woman off to Spain on his bicycle where they lived happily ever after, or so the story sounded to my young ears.

As a child, I used to wonder how exactly a grown man and woman, complete with luggage and a generous supply of onions could actually cycle from rural Lincolnshire to sunny Spain, but I guess where romance is concerned, anything is possible. My mother never heard from her friend again, but she did once receive word from another friend that the young woman eventually married the onion seller and made her home in Spain, where the happy couple bred a new generation of onion sellers.

As I listened to our musical onion seller disappearing down the road in his battered vehicle, I wondered, fleetingly, if this young man could somehow be a descendent of my mother's onion seller? I guess, where romance is concerned, anything is possible.

The Englishman, the Irishman and the Scotsman

The experiences that come from living in another country mean that, very quickly, we are put in a position when we learn more about ourselves. Characteristics that we learn to associate with those from other nations are usually quickly dispelled and, hopefully, we begin to learn more about people of other faiths, cultures and those who speak a different language.

It is very easy to fall into the trap of national stereotypes, such as Germans being efficient and hardworking, the Spanish having a mañana attitude to life, the Italians being lazy and too fond of pasta, never to trust a Dutch businessman, and the French who are great lovers, dress nicely, but are just so unreliable. Some elements of national characteristics may relate to some people, but it is wrong to typecast a whole nation with the same attributes. Yet, as we are currently witnessing with some of the jingoistic debates about immigration in the UK, and the current popularity of right-wing political parties, such prejudices are alive and well.

As with so many moving to Spain, we initially looked for British people for support to help us with building, electrical, plumbing and legal work. However, we quickly learned that in many cases it was our own countrymen that were the most likely to rip off newcomers. My work as a newspaper reporter brought me in close contact with many Brits who had been conned by fellow Brits, and I learned very

---

55

quickly that there was no love lost between people when it came to earning a fast euro. Of course, this is a wide generalisation, because there were also many who would go out of their way to help others. However, most learned quickly that it is not the nationality of your neighbours that is important; it is how they treat you.

Our first experience was with an English electrician who arrived at our new home to install lighting. He arrived, endlessly chewing gum, with no ladder or even a screwdriver, which we had to borrow from neighbours before he could start the job. Our Scottish plumber was no better, although he did arrive with a spanner to fix a leaking tap. He broke the pipe and our new kitchen was flooded.

Most would think that we had learned the errors of our ways, but we were naive and simply put the incidents down to bad luck. However, it was our dealings with an Irishman called Connor (a clue is in the name) that were possibly the most worrying.

Connor, an Irishman, came highly recommended from neighbours to start work on our small swimming pool. He was a charming man, full of amusing stories, and displayed a knowledge of swimming pools that, to the unenlightened, was impressive. He had an annoying catch phrase of "No Stress, no Mess", which he kept repeating at the end of most of his sentences. Connor assured us that our new pool would be built to the highest quality standards, and planning permissions would be obtained and completed in four weeks. We duly handed over a significant sum of money as a deposit to pay for materials, and waited for the work to start.

Three months later we were still waiting for Connor to arrive. Sadly, his phone had by then been disconnected, he was not living at the address given and no one had seen him in recent weeks. Our neighbours were full of apologies, and we finally gave up all hope of ever having a swimming pool.

A further three months later, a slimmer Connor arrived on our doorstep. He was full of apologies, and as charming as ever. It seemed that it had all been a case of mistaken identity relating to an issue with a ride on a lawn mower that had landed him into serious trouble with the police. Mistaken identity or not, Connor had enjoyed a six month stay in accommodation at His Majesty's Pleasure, and appeared duly chastened by the experience.

Readers who have spent an evening in a bar with an Irishman telling stories over a glass or two of Guinness will recognise that after a period, one's brain closes down into a form of gentle submission. Connor assured us that our money was safe and that our pool would be started the following day and completed within one month.

True to his word, Connor arrived the following day with two men and started digging. Four weeks later, our new pool was completed, which we were pleased with. We paid the remaining money due to Connor and, apart from worrying about whether planning permission had ever been actually granted, we continued to enjoy the pool until it developed a major leak, which is a story for another time.

The moral of this story is that we now have more open minds about nationalities that can get the job done. We quickly learned not to rely on British electricians, plumbers and builders, but to use those who can do the job at a reasonable price, regardless of nationality. Nowadays, we use a German plumber, a Canarian electrician, a Spanish builder and a Moroccan decorator. Our dentist is Argentinean and our favourite bar is owned and run by Romanians. Sadly, there are no Welshmen in this story.

The Charter Trip

Readers who know Gran Canaria well may have spotted what looks like the rusting hulk of a plane near the main road near Bahia Feliz. No, it is not the latest acquisition by my least favourite airline, or one that failed to land at the right airport, but part of a film set. More about the plane later.

We tend to forget that popular tourism in the Canary Islands in general, and Gran Canaria specifically, is a relatively modern phenomena. Certainly, influential and wealthy Europeans would visit Las Palmas in Gran Canaria, where its beautiful Las Canteras Beach was a popular destination for the few cruise ships that plied the Atlantic before the two World Wars and the Spanish Civil War.

Despite the opening of Gran Canaria's Gando Airport in 1930, it was only in the 1950s that Gran Canaria would begin to receive significant numbers of tourists; not from the UK, but from Scandinavia. During Christmas 1957, the Swedish airline, Transair AB, organised a flight to Gran Canaria with all of its 54 seats occupied. This was an historic moment, since it was the first flight of the new charter market and the beginning of the mass tourism market that Gran Canaria enjoys today.

Gran Canaria has always been popular with the Scandinavian tourist industry, which continues to the present day. The island is also a very popular destination for German tourists, although its popularity has strengthened and waned over the years according to the German economy. During the

59

reunification of Germany and changes to taxation laws, many German residents could not afford to maintain their homes on the island, with many returning home, together with an accompanying reduction in tourists. Surprisingly, Brits, in general, have always favoured Tenerife, but with its more discerning tourists heading to Gran Canaria, Lanzarote and Fuerteventura.

Back to the rusting hulk of a plane, just off the main road near Bahia Feliz. Despite its age, the plane still looks impressive when seen at close hand. It has an interesting story, because it was featured in a Swedish film called Sällskapsresan in the 1980s. The film was later released in English as 'The Charter Trip'. Over the years, the film has achieved something of a cult status with over 2.5 million people watching the film, making it the biggest cinema success in Sweden to date.

The film is about "a stuffy and nerdy Swede", who has a fear of flying, who arrives in the fictional town of Nueva Estocolmo in Gran Canaria. The film involves smuggling money in a loaf of bread, an alcoholic duo, as well as some Swedish jokes that do not always translate well. You can find extracts of the film on YouTube; do watch it if you can.

The plane, as well as the film, is a worthy reminder of the early days of tourism on the island. Although tourism as we currently know it, had a shaky start, the popularity of all of the Canary Islands, and the prosperity that it has brought to the islands over the years could be said to have begun with that single charter plane flight and 54 passengers from Sweden.

The Case of the Noisy Dominoes

We live in a noisy world, and the opportunity to find near silence from time to time is a welcome and refreshing one. A recent report from the World Health Organisation claims that Spain is the noisiest country in Europe. Apparently noise levels are around 70 decibels, whereas the World Health Organisation recommends a maximum of 55db during the day and 45 db at night.

These figures do not surprise me. As much as I like most Spanish people, and generalisations are dangerous, I have always maintained that Spanish babies are born with their volume controls glued to the maximum loud position, and it stays that way for life.

Travelling by bus, train, sitting in the theatre, dentist, hospital or doctor's surgery surrounded by "Silence" notices, always makes me smile. No chance; whenever a group of Spanish people get together they do what they like doing best, and that is to talk, and the louder the better.

One of my favourite Spanish cities, Seville, has decided to take action against excessive noise, and decided to ban the playing of dominoes and dice games in outdoor cafes! Well, yes, I guess it is a step in the right direction, but I can think of any number of 'calming' measures without banning elderly men, in particular, enjoying playing dominoes in the sunshine.

How about excessive revving of motorcycle and car engines? Loud televisions in cafes, bars and restaurants, as well as all night singing and dancing in residential areas? I would also add fireworks, be it a Church organised show of devotion to a particular saint during religious processions, or the endless explosion of fireworks from Halloween to January 6th each year, which terrifies most creatures living outdoors, as well as many people.

Seville is also looking to ban the rolling of barrels down streets and, strangely enough, drinking and eating whilst standing outside cafe bars and terraces. This new law, like some of Spain's other strange laws, such as noisy stag parties, and pianists playing loudly at home have led perpetrators to face prosecution. The new Seville law, like many others are often part of local democracy, voted upon by local neighbourhood associations and brought into law without too much consideration of the consequences.

Now to the real cause of all this noise. It is simple; it is mostly from noisy people. Interestingly, Spanish doctors report that around 7 per cent of all Spaniards have serious problems with their vocal cords, and among teachers the figure rises to nearly one in four, making it one of the main reasons why they take a day off work, as well as being one of the reasons why I usually avoid entering a Spanish classroom. World Voice Day, on 16 April, is when Spanish doctors spring into action to remind the public as to why they may suffer from throat problems, which also includes too much smoking. Sadly, those poor vocal chords stand no chance.

My message to Seville is simple; leave those poor domino and dice throwing players alone. They really are not doing any harm. How about encouraging everyone to speak a little quieter and to actually listen to what other people are saying, rather than speaking over them? This particular piece of advice would apply to many other nationalities too.

Family and Community Matter

Many living in Spain fail to recognise the importance of family and community to the Spanish people. Unlike many Northern European countries, where the sick and elderly are shipped off to hospitals, care homes and hospices, it is still the culture in many Mediterranean countries that families generally take care of their own.

I often receive complaints from those living in Spain about the overall care in both National Health, as well as private hospitals. Complaints are rarely about the quality of medical care, which by all accounts, could not be higher in any part of Europe. However, there is a heavy reliance upon family and close friends to provide basic nursing and aftercare following surgery. Cleaning and washing patients, providing some food and feeding patients is usually carried out by close family members, unlike hospitals in the UK, Germany and Sweden, where this kind of care is normally regarded as basic nursing and included within hospital care.

Much of this family and community care is down to culture. In Spain, for instance, family groups provide care at all stages of life, with the family acting as a kind of safety net. From the birth of a baby to the last days of a much-loved grandparent has traditionally been the responsibility of the immediate family. Grandparents are usually on hand to assist with bringing up the children of their sons and daughters, with plenty of aunts and uncles to act as baby-sitters along the way. When grandparents, or indeed great grandparents become too ill or frail to care for themselves, it is the younger members of the family who are expected to take care of them.

In the Canary Islands, many parents are in their teens when they give birth. It is customary for the young couple to live with one of the couple's parents until the time comes for them to find a home of their own. Traditionally, properties have been extended, garages turned into apartments, or another floor added to a dwelling to provide a home for the young couple. In time, it is the parents who, as grandparents, move into the garage, annex or roof conversion and it is the turn of the young couple to take over the family home.

Of course in recent years, following the many problems created by the economic recession, the pattern has changed, particularly in cities and urban areas. Family members have had to travel further from their home towns and villages to find work, and this kind of family and community care is no longer possible. As a result, there are more family breakdowns and single parents than there have been in previous generations. Social attitudes to religion have also changed in the last ten years or so, with many Spaniards admitting that they no longer attend church. This is something that would have been unthinkable in the past, but was all part of the hidden community and social adhesive, which held families and communities together. However, in rural communities, villages and the islands, little has changed.

This pattern of community and family life tends to create problems, and is often the reason why those who are sick, elderly and frail do not find the support that they need later in life. It is simply not built into the system. The care from medical centres and hospitals will probably be very good, but do not expect to find a Macmillan nurse available to assist in matters relating to end of life or cancer related illness. There are few hospices to deal with end-of-life care, and those that do exist are mostly run by religious orders.

It is important that everyone should consider the options open to them later in life and to make appropriate provision, and not to expect your adopted country to look after you. They will do their best, but it may not be what you would expect from the country of your birth in your final years. It is yet another reminder that living in the sun means not only sipping gin and tonics on the beach, but accepting and adjusting to the customs and traditions of your newly adopted country - warts and all.

Runways or Community?

Visitors to the island of Gran Canaria are often surprised to learn that the island hosts the third largest airport in Spain. Due to the rapidly increasing popularity of the island as an attractive and successful tourist destination, the airport has, until recently, been close to maximum capacity. Over the last few years, a programme of refurbishment, redevelopment and extension has taken place to ensure that the airport retains its prestige position and meets the needs of the island. Indeed, over the last few days, an impressive new terminal building has been opened, but the one thing that is still missing is a second runway, which is needed in order to absorb increased capacity of flights, as well as larger aircraft.

A second runway has been planned since 2001, but the downside was that it would necessitate the demolition of an entire Canarian village, Ojos de Garza. Needless to say, the villagers were not too impressed with the plans and embarked upon a series of disruption for many years in an attempt to persuade developers that they should build the second runway elsewhere. On a small island, the choices are limited, but the villagers were determined to ensure that their views were fully taken into account.

Legal battles, hunger strikes, marches and disobedience have followed over the years, with the 5000 villagers remaining united against both the threats and temptations thrown at them. Most of the residents refused to sell their properties to the developers since it would be difficult to buy new homes on the island. They wished to remain as a community and stay together.

Since the end of the Second World War, the UK has seen social problems as a result of mistakes made by well meaning planners and architects who demolished what were regarded as terraced 'slums' in favour of high-rise flats. Many such monstrosities were built in cities across the UK, as well as in other parts of Europe. As well as disregarding the need for green space, and play areas for children, many planners forgot that community cohesion is the essential component for any society to thrive. Disrupting neighbourhoods and tearing whole communities apart from their neighbours, extended families and friends may have made economic and commercial sense at the time, but failed to take account of community needs and the provision of mutual support.

For many years, the people of Ojos de Garza have been unable to move home, because no one wanted to buy their properties. Mortgages could not be obtained from the banks since the properties were deemed to be worthless. Thankfully, their determination and perseverance has forced the planners and authorities to think again.

A solution has finally been found, with developers agreeing to rebuild their homes in a new location, two kilometres away from their existing village. The airport management company, Aena, has agreed to build an entirely new village, which will be a copy of the original, and both locals and the management of the airport are happy with the arrangement. After years of indecision and argument, work on the new runway can begin and is scheduled to be completed by 2025, but only after the villagers of Ojos de Garza get their new village and their existing homes can finally be demolished.

Yes, the airport does need another runway, but at what cost to family and community? These villagers have demonstrated that the value of community, which is very much an intrinsic part of the Canarian and Spanish psyche, is important to them and that their views deserve to be taken into account. Maybe other towns and cities in Europe could learn a little from their example, and the mistakes of tearing communities apart in the past, at the whim of architects and developers, will not be repeated.

The Water Boys and the Orange Man

I clearly remember the daily deliveries of bread and milk to our home when I was growing up in rural Lincolnshire. However, over time, many of these much-valued services ceased on the grounds that they were no longer economic to operate. Local shops and small supermarkets were supposed to take over this much valued local service, and the days of the milkman and bread man's daily deliveries now seem to be a thing of the past in many of the UK's towns and villages.

Although we do not receive daily milk deliveries in Gran Canaria, many homes still receive a range of other welcome local deliveries of essential products. At broadly the same time each week, the dogs in our road begin to create a commotion. It is a cacophony of angry barking, designed to let humans know that intruders are approaching. The barking begins at the top of our road, and passes from dog to dog down the road until our dog, Bella, picks up the urgent signal, which cruelly disturbs her from her slumbers, forcing her to join in and pass on the message in her shrillest possible bark. Why all the fuss? Of course, it is the water boys delivering supplies of mineral water to those homes that have ordered it.

Although we have water delivered to our home in large bottles, it is often amusing to see a large pipe being dragged into buildings from a tanker in order to fill up a collection of not too clean looking reusable containers. Often the inhabitants are not at home, and the water boys have to return two or three times before they can complete their delivery and collect their money. It is a time consuming process, but as most people sensibly drink mineral water rather than tap water, it is an essential part of everyday life.

We also receive regular visits from local farmers offering their current range of produce; often it is freshly picked tomatoes, bananas or onions, and sometimes vegetables that we have never seen or tried before. Occasionally we will try these unusual offerings, but only after the farmer has told us how to prepare and cook them. It is usually possible to identify which farmer is visiting simply by the sound of their vehicle or horn; one farmer even plays a tin whistle to alert potential customers of his arrival.

The latest addition to our fruit and vegetable service is the Orange Man, as many locals call him. He parks his van just outside our village on most days of the week, always offering a cheery greeting to all who pass by. His small van contains a treasure trove of fresh fruit, which is a delight to the eye. Plump, juicy oranges, boxes of ripe, sweet apricots, strawberries and cherries are all on offer from his and his neighbour's local smallholdings. The Orange Man readily offers samples of his produce for his customers to try before purchase, and I doubt many leave him empty handed. Inevitably, we buy far more fruit than we originally intended, but the prices are so reasonable that it is difficult to ignore.

Fresh bread and bottled gas are also delivered regularly in our village, as well as bottled water from a range of competing companies from Tenerife, and even from the Peninsular. However, the economics of such a journey, as well as the carbon footprint does raise many questions about the wisdom of such long distance deliveries.

Home delivery services in the UK now appear to have morphed into a weekly delivery service from an out-of-town supermarket, together with a steep delivery charge. However, time and economics have yet to catch up with the islands, and we still enjoy regular, local delivery services, which are invaluable to the local community, and particularly for those working, the sick, elderly and disabled. Long may home deliveries continue.

Risk Assessments

The
Canary
Islander

On the Beat

I'm often asked about policing in Spain and the Canary Islands and how it compares with that in the UK. I usually avoid writing about policing issues, as much is subjective and depends upon personal experiences and encounters with the law. However, based on my work as a journalist, as well as many reports and comments received, maybe now is the time to deal with the issue.

For me, the question came to the fore during my recent visit to the UK. My partner and I had found a wallet in Dorchester, the county town of Dorset, during a very brief stopover in the town. From a quick glance, I could see that the wallet contained over 100 pounds, bank cards and the usual clutter of a man's wallet. Time was short and so we went to the local police station to hand it over as lost property. To my surprise, I found that the police station was only open three days each week and closed for lunch between 13.00 and 14.00. Sadly, we had arrived ten minutes late, and even though there were police cars in the car park and voices could be heard inside the building, no one would answer our knocks on the door and there was no letterbox to drop off the wallet. Although I am aware that the Dorset police headquarters is based in a remote part of the county, I was surprised that the county town could not offer a better service to its community. After all, community policing, in my view, is not just about catching criminals in fast cars, but also assisting the community when it is most needed.

To avoid further delays, I opened the wallet and examined it more fully. Maybe I could return the wallet to one of the banks that had issued the cards in the wallet? Fortunately, tucked inside, I found a driving licence. I could see from the licence that it and the wallet belonged to an elderly man, and it was clear that I had to get the wallet to him as soon as possible.

With the help of GPS on my mobile phone, we located the elderly man's home, where we quickly realised that our efforts and delay in our travel plans were not in vain. This frail and worried gentleman was being helped by his young neighbour to call the police to report the lost wallet, and he beamed with relief and delight when we returned the wallet to him.

This experience made me realise how fortunate that we are to have the police service in the Canary Islands. It seems that we are never far away from a police officer, be it local, National or the Civil Guard. I personally have always found them to be courteous and professional in my dealings with them, both as a journalist, as well as a citizen. Frankly, I feel safer in the Canary Islands than I can remember experiencing in the UK. During my two weeks in the UK, with the exception of police officers at the airport, I only saw two police officers dealing with a single incident in the city of Bristol. The usual response to such criticism is, of course budget cuts and the recession, but I suggest that the safety of its community is the main responsibility of any government, and even though the weather was very cold during my visit, maybe a few more police officers on patrol would be of greater benefit than hiding in large warm offices in rural Dorset? Just a thought.

It was just one of those days

It was just one of those days. You will all know what I mean when I say this, as we all have them from time to time. It was one of those days when something that might have been relatively straightforward in the UK, could potentially turn into an expensive nightmare. Most will empathise with those situations where one feels particularly vulnerable, mostly due to language and cultural differences. Indeed, it was the kind of day when I began to wish that I had turned right instead of left…

One second I was driving down a one-way village street, and the next, there was a loud thud and unhealthy sounding scrape, as a car reversed into my car. Of course, it is important to recognise the priorities of life, first of all; thankfully no one was hurt, but I was a little taken aback when I saw the woman driver in the offending car shaking her fist at me. I got out of the car, and I could see that the only thing that the woman had hurt was her pride. I was also a little taken aback when I saw her briefly brush her hair and check her lips and mascara, before she got out of the car. Hmm, maybe she thought I would ask her out on a date afterwards.

Once the problem that she had caused had sunk in, the woman eventually got out of her car and poured a babble of a language that I did not understand over me. It was a language I did not recognise as English, French, German or Spanish, but I have always found mime to be an incredibly useful addition to any language. I looked at her car, where I could see minor damage to the front wing. My car seemed to have got the worst of the incident, as not only was the rear wing damaged, but the two doors also had suffered nasty scrapes and dents to the paintwork.

She was not a young woman, but stylish to a fault. From her gestures I could work out that she wanted my insurance details. No problem, but she appeared reluctant to give me hers in return. I had learned a long time ago that this was never the time to apportion blame or to expect an apology. However, I did insist upon receiving all her details in return, although I was a little alarmed that she could not find her own insurance details. It was at this point that I began to wonder if she actually had any insurance.

By now a large crowd had gathered around our two cars. With unemployment being so high in the village, there was no shortage of spectators, together with offers of help and advice; after all, Canarians are very friendly and gregarious people. I began to wonder if this situation could get difficult but, to my surprise, several members of the gathered crowd were urging the flustered woman to give me her details, although she could not find the insurance document in the car. Eventually, I could see that there was no point in pressing her further, took her name and address, car registration company, as well as the name of the insurance company that she thought she was insured with. I also took several photos of the damage with my phone, and went on my way.

A quick telephone call to my own insurance company later made me grateful for selecting a Spanish company that had an English-speaking department to assist me. Although now relatively confident in speaking Spanish, I always recommend that in matters, medical, legal and financial, and unless one is totally confident in the language, it is wise to involve a professional translator. It was for this reason that I had selected a company that could communicate with me in perfect English. Within minutes, all the details had been confirmed, I was directed to a local car body repairer and reassured that whatever the situation with the other driver's insurance, that I would be fully covered at no cost to myself. I could not have wished for better service.

One week later and I have now collected my vehicle from the body repair shop, and it looks almost as good as new. The strange thing was that two weeks earlier, someone else had crashed into the wing on the other side of my car. Maybe someone just wanted me to have a matching pair?

Dogs

As a dog lover, the way that dogs and other animals are treated in Spain often distresses me. As far as dogs are concerned, with the help from residents from other countries, much has been learned about animal welfare, and although the number of dogs abandoned each year remains at appalling high levels, in my experience, cases of cruelty are now being listened to and usually acted upon, although there remain some distressing exceptions.

A few days ago, I received an email from Pat, an Irish woman living in Spain's Costa del Sol. Pat and her partner, Paul, had been walking their small terrier, Susie, on some waste land earlier in the day. This was something that the couple did once or twice each day, because although they lived in a villa, it was small and lacked enough space for a lively terrier to chase around in. Susie, a friendly, but not the most reliable of dogs, was chasing her ball at the end of a long extending lead, when a large German Shepherd dog appeared and began to attack the small dog. Paul ran after Susie, and quickly picked up the small dog, who was bleeding around her neck and front legs and was clearly in some pain. The German Shepherd then began to viciously attack Paul, who was still holding Susie, and knocked him to the ground.

Pat was frantic and was calling for help as she tried to beat the dog off Paul and Susie with her large handbag. Eventually, the owner of the German Shepherd appeared, called the dog, but it ignored her. Other dog walkers appeared and rushed to help the struggling couple. Eventually the German Shepherd was pulled off Paul by its German owner, leaving Paul badly injured with severe lacerations to his arm, legs and face.

The incident was reported to the police, the owner tracked down and the German Shepherd was destroyed. Paul spent two days in hospital, not only recovering from severe bites, but also a reoccurrence of his heart condition. Susie remained in the veterinary hospital receiving treatment for severe lacerations, with some doubt as to whether one of her legs will function properly again. Meanwhile, the German owner of the dog faces prosecution, as well as a large claim for damages.

This incident reminds me of several attacks by dogs that I too have witnessed. Many people live in small apartments or small properties, wish to have a dog and often purchase one that grows to a far bigger size than originally intended, or the 'macho' thing creeps in whereby they just have to have a big dog, regardless of the fact that they have no outdoor space, and are too lazy to exercise it regularly. Many dogs, of all sizes, lack regular walks and exercise and, as a result, have an abundance of pent up energy and frustration that causes the kind of trouble experienced by Pat and Paul. As Pat said, it was not the fault of the dog, but the fault of the owners.

The message from this distressing story is clear, unless you wish to be faced with a large claim for damages and injury, or the distress of having your dog destroyed, don't get a large one if you live in an apartment, or any dog, come to that. If you must have a dog, make sure that you can look after it, ensure that it is exercised regularly and don't leave it on its own in an apartment barking all day. If you cannot do this, get stick insects.

Tyre Safety

Recently witnessing a nasty accident on the motorway in Gran Canaria, where fortunately all the passengers survived unscathed, made me ask some questions about the cause. Apparently, one tyre had exploded, which was due to the age of the tyre and failure of the rubber.

For me, this was an unknown phenomenon. Although I am careful about regularly checking the depth of tyre tread from time to time, and changing a tyre when necessary, I frankly had no idea that tyres 'age' and that rubber deteriorates. Judging from conversations with others, most did not know this either.

We have a second vehicle, which is not heavily used and, since we live on an island, has very low mileage, because there are few long distances that can be travelled. The vehicle is parked on the road outside our home, and I have to admit that, for much of the day, it is parked in the full glare of the sun. The tyres all look as good as new, but I took the car to the tyre depot for a check - just in case.

Jorge, the mechanic, looked horrified when he pointed out that the tyres were made in 2005, as a coding that represents the date is clearly inscribed on the tyres. With, not undisguised delight, Jorge went on to point out some deterioration of the rubber, as well as unevenness on the walls of the tyres. He made that inward sucking of breath that people make when they are about to impart bad news. I prepared myself. They were not exactly bulges, Jorge explained, but they were heading that way. Jorge then went on to show me a tyre that had exploded, and inferred that the same would happen to me unless I bought a new set of tyres. The exploded tyre was not a pleasant sight, but it did help me to understand the problem.

Apparently, the performance of tyres deteriorates with age, because they contain anti-oxidising chemicals to slow the rate of ageing, but they need to be in use to be effective. My low mileage vehicle was deteriorating on the roadside, and because of the intensity of the sun and heat, the ageing process was accelerated, making the tyres unroadworthy. Low mileage, older cars tend to be at most risk from premature ageing, explained Jorge, continuing with a sharp intake of breath and shaking his head.

Of course, the age of a tyre and when it should be replaced depends upon many factors, but Jorge reckons that 6 years is about the age limit in a hot country. Living on an island, we also have a particular problem in that tyres rarely reach the end of their life based upon the depth of tread alone. Distances tend to be short and residents, retired or otherwise, do not travel very far in a year.

Jorge pointed out that the date that tyres are made is clearly inscribed on the wall of the tyre, in the form of four numbers. These numbers indicate the year and week number that it was made; for example 2612 will be week 26 of 2012. This information can also be used to ensure that you are buying tyres with the longest shelf life possible.

Jorge had successfully made his point and I reluctantly agreed to buy four new tyres. I handed over my credit card, but I am now pleased that I did so since tyres are the only contact that there is between the driver and the perils of the motorway. I think it was a good investment.

The La Palma Megatsunami

I'm off to the Canarian island of La Palma, which is also known as 'The Beautiful Island', again next week. Although I live on the island of Gran Canaria, all of the seven main islands that make up this fascinating archipelago are very different to each other. I try to visit each island from time to time, but I am particularly fond of La Palma, which is the fifth largest of the seven main islands, covering an area of around 706 square kilometres, with a population of around 90,000 people, most of whom live in the island's capital city of Santa Cruz de la Palma.

It is a lush, green and wooded island, with beautiful forests, and is a walker's paradise. Clear skies make this island a stargazer's paradise too, which is one of the reasons that a number of international telescopes operate on the island to monitor the night skies. The island offers the most diverse plant life of all the Canary Islands, together with species such as the La Palma Giant Lizard, La Palma Chaffinch, Quail and Goldcrest, all of which are unique to the island. Since 1983, the island has been one of the UNESCO World Network of Biosphere Reserves. Should tourists wish to escape sun seekers heading for the beaches on the larger islands, this is the place to come.

As with all the Canary Islands, La Palma is volcanic in origin, with the volcano rising to around 7km (4 miles) above the floor of the Atlantic Ocean. The island was formed around 4 million years ago, and is one of the most volcanically active of all the Canary Islands, and this is where the problems begin...

It has been suggested by some that one day, far into the future, La Palma will be the cause of one of the largest tsunamis that the world has ever known. Indeed, to clarify its awesome status, it has been referred to as a megatsunami in waiting. This is based on the hypothesis that rising pressure caused part of Cumbre Vieja, which is a volcanic ridge in the south of the island, to slip towards the Atlantic Ocean and that during a future volcanic eruption, part of it would slip into the Atlantic. Currently, the Cumbre Vieja is dormant, with the last eruption taking place in 1971.

Should the worst occur, it has been speculated that the resulting megatsunami would create a giant wave of around 49 metres (160ft) causing devastation along the Atlantic coastlines of North America, wiping out New York, the Caribbean and the north coast of South America, as well as affecting an area of around 25 km (16 miles) inland from the coast. From the moment that part of La Palma falls into the Atlantic there will be a period of about 6 to 8 hours before it hits the American coastline. In any case, should the worst happen, it is not supposed to happen for another ten thousand years or so, which should allow plenty of time to move home.

I should also make it clear that many eminent scientists and geologists have refuted this theory as pure hype, and claim that La Palma is stable and will not fall into the sea. It is claimed that this is a disaster theory invented by researchers intent on gaining funding for their own research projects. Others claim that this is a convenient story exaggerated by US insurance companies, intent on raising insurance premiums, as well as being seen as a business opportunity by the hazard industry. Even if the worst should happen, there would hardly be more than a splash felt at the other side of the Atlantic, and so New Yorkers should continue to feel safe.

There's nothing like a good disaster story is there? After all, we all flock to the movies to see them. However, when it is closer to real life, it is not quite so entertaining. This story has already created many victims. Questions were asked in the British Parliament following a BBC television programme that first revealed the danger, many Americans considered selling up and moving to higher ground, tourists cancelled holidays to La Palma, many sold their homes on the island and a number charter flights to the island ceased.

As for me, I cannot wait to visit and explore the island once again. However, I will make sure that I do not jump up and down too energetically when I get to Cumbre Vieja - just in case!

The Big TV Switch Off

Nothing disturbs the mind of an otherwise dedicated resident than being unable to watch their favourite TV programmes from their home country.

Admittedly, in countries such as Spain, France, Portugal and Italy, watching a good dose of national TV from time to time does help to improve language skills. Indeed, I know of several residents who claim that they have learned their new language entirely from watching television and listening to the radio in their adopted countries.

Sadly, I doubt that this could be true in the case of Spain, where reality TV, quizzes and game shows seem to dominate the daily diet. The daily output is a little weird, although many of the news channels are usually worth watching. There is also much to be said from watching familiar Hollywood blockbusters with Spanish subtitles; it is a good way to become more familiar with the language and is much cheaper than buying Spanish lessons.

Over the years, I have noticed that even the most hardened and cynical critics of the BBC, such as those who detest paying the annual licence fee and would previously have supported an end to the national broadcaster, have now recognised that it has become a national institution. I have seen residents beg for British television and crave to be able to pay the licence fee after just a few weeks in Spain. I have witnessed grown men cry when their beloved Sky box and enormous dish become obsolete overnight when the broadcaster transferred to another satellite. I have seen usually law-abiding Brits happily hand over fistfuls of cash to known Mafia enterprises, simply for the privileged of having a baking tray looking 'aerial' fitted to their roof, together with an assurance that they will receive Brit television for life, albeit illegally gathered from broadcasters in the UK.

It is certainly true, although many residents will be reluctant to admit it, that being able to watch familiar television programmes from their home country makes for a happier life. Of course, purists will say that this is wrong; they should suffer the delights of Spanish TV like everyone else, and be out eating paella and drinking Rioja every evening; they should be socialising with Spanish people, and spending their time getting to know the culture and language. Of course, they are right, philosophically and culturally speaking; however, this view ignores the fact that British television is of exceedingly high quality, keeps Brits in touch with their language and culture and, perhaps most importantly of all, helps to maintain links with the country of their birth. Above all they happen to enjoy it; indeed, it is best described as a soggy comfort blanket.

Over the last few weeks, one national UK newspaper has had a campaign that appears to attempt to undermine life in Spain, Portugal and France in favour of a new El Dorado in the making - that of Dubai. Personally, I cannot see Dot and Bert from Wigan dreaming of retiring in Dubai, and certainly not opening a bar there. I suspect that vested interests are at work at the newspaper, and they are desperately trying to sell homes for a Sheik or two. The newspaper claims that 20 per cent of all British residents are leaving Spain "in droves" because of the recession, unemployment and a host of other reasons, although they forget to mention, of course, that 80 per cent of residents choose to stay and are rather content with their lives.

The paper has it completely wrong. The real reason behind the "exodus" from Spain to the UK is nothing more complicated than television transmission from the previous satellite has suddenly ended; it is now much more difficult to receive British television in Spain that it was a few months ago. There are currently huge swathes of residents foaming at the mouth that they can no longer receive Brit TV, and this is the real reason for their sudden change of heart and a move back to the UK. Sorry, but I must end now, Eastenders is about to start.

Buying or Renting?

The World recession has changed attitudes to many issues. For those intending to start a new life in Spain, the option of buying a home before the recession, possibly with a cheap Spanish mortgage was always a tempting one. Good value properties were readily and cheaply available, and mortgages were never too much of a problem to obtain, particularly if you had the right contacts. Of course, this was part of the problem, as Spain and other Mediterranean countries have since found out. As a result, many properties are often difficult to sell, many are in negative equity and mortgage foreclosures are a common occurrence, with many returning to their countries of origin, bitter and dejected.

One of the questions that I am frequently asked by those planning to move abroad is "Should I buy or rent a home in Spain?" Many would-be travellers have listened to horror stories from those returning or read in one of the Brit tabloids about the "horrors of buying a home in Spain" that advise not to buy. "Never buy, always rent" has become the current mantra for some people, and voiced particularly loudly by those who still have a property to sell. However, this is not always the best advice, and I would caution against taking such advice too seriously.

A high percentage of emails that I receive relate to circumstances where things have gone badly wrong in the rental market. Short-term rentals now seem to be the order of the day and if you decide to rent, be prepared to move frequently. Many landlords are speculative and only want to rent out properties during the 'off peak' season and like to move tenants on in time to make higher rentals during the main holiday period. Neither do landlords currently like tenants to feel too 'comfortable'. Many have been badly bitten during the financial crisis with unpaid rents and are cautiously against allowing long-term tenancies. Many do not speak the language fluently enough to check the conditions of their tenancy agreements, which should always be checked by a competent and reliable Spanish lawyer; however, select one who can advise you in your own language.

Of course, much depends upon personal circumstances, including whether or not you have the capital or mortgage capability to buy a home in Spain; if not, renting is the only available option. Maybe you are retired, have a home in the UK and intend to return in the future, in which case renting maybe the best idea. However, if you intend to make a commitment to your new country and are prepared to accept the advantages, as well as the challenges, then buying a home would always be my preferred option. There is nothing quite like owning your own home, albeit with the help of a mortgage. However, this is on the basis that you do your homework thoroughly first.

If you intend to buy, my advice would be to live in rented accommodation in an area where you plan to buy for a year or two. This is to ensure that you actually like the location, as well as giving you plenty of time to look for available properties in an area that you intend to make your permanent home. Look for bargains, bank forced sales, as well as talking to neighbours and friends. By all means, check out the local estate agents as a good source of information but in most cases, it is the locals who know about the best local deals.

Whatever the cynics say, it is still relatively easy to obtain a bank mortgage in Spain, particularly if you are working. Speak to several banks, lawyers, developers and people that you know. Remember, that it is still often a case of 'who' you know and not 'what' you know in Spain. When the time comes to buy, look for a reputable Spanish lawyer. Make sure it is someone well known and recommended to you by friends and neighbours.

If you do decide to buy a property, make sure it is for the right reasons. Before the financial crisis, I knew many who would buy properties for a 'song', often on unregistered land, hoping to make a large profit when it came to sell the property several months on. Many such speculators were caught out, and this is why so many are currently bitterly against purchasing properties in Spain. Don't let their greed put you off. Remember that you are primarily buying a home and it shouldn't matter too much if its value rises or falls, particularly in the short term.

If you still have a property in the UK, lucky you, because it should provide you with some spare cash to get the new home that you are really looking for. However, don't keep your old home just in case you wish to return. If you are moving on a temporary flight of fancy, then it may be wise to keep it for a few months. However, if you are aiming for a permanent life in a new country, my best advice is to cut the umbilical cord and move on. If you should return later, so many things will have changed, that you probably won't like your old home and neighbours anyway! It is always best to move on and never to look back. I have known many residents who fret so much about their old home, which is either left empty or let to strangers, that they are never able to let go and move on, and enjoy the real purpose of their new lives in the sun.

Enchanted Islands

The
Canary
Islander

Escape to La Palma

La Palma? No, I don't mean La Palma de Majorca or Las Palmas de Gran Canaria, but a little known island paradise, which is one of the seven islands (or maybe it is 8, depending upon your definition of an island, and political persuasions) that together make up the Canarian archipelago.

The island is the fifth largest of all the Canary Islands and many would say it is the most beautiful of all the islands. I happily subscribe to its affectionate title of 'La Isla Bonita' (The Beautiful Island). The island is 68 miles (126 km) from Tenerife, but don't worry, because it is nothing like its larger, brash neighbour, and there are few tourists to bother about either, other than those walking, star gazing and enjoying a natural, unspoiled environment.

I am very fond of all the Canary Islands; each one is unique and has its own charms, as well as offering a unique perspective on life. However, if like me, you enjoy lush green grass, forests, woodlands, flowers, blue sky and unpolluted air, and a climate that is best described as an 'eternal spring', then this island is for you. It is a picturesque place that is beautifully maintained, and the streets are clean with no graffiti or dog excreta to be seen.

Despite the current financial climate and troubling unemployment situation in the Canary Islands, this island still gives the impression of being rather prosperous. Unlike some of its neighbours, properties appear well cared for, gardens are trimmed and buildings well painted and maintained. Cruise ships come and go, depositing hoards of gannet-like tourists each morning ready to gobble up the local delicacies on offer. However, by mid afternoon travel weary passengers return to their floating palaces ready to set sail for another day and a brief stop at yet another destination. Most seem to be unaware of where they are as they trudge reluctantly behind the tour guide, taking endless photographs that no one will ever see. After their departure, an air of calm settles over the island as the locals resume a steadier pace of life.

A regular and reliable bus service operates throughout the island, and although the timings are best described as 'Canarian', the bus does eventually turn up. Pretty little shelters mark the bus stops that are painted bright yellow with an orange tiled roof; complete with bus timetable and a terracotta pot for cigarette stubs. Passengers should be tolerant that the driver may need to stop the bus briefly in the forest in order to empty his bladder. After all it is a long journey with many twists and turns to negotiate. Just sit in the bus patiently and watch the lizards sunbathing at the side of the road, whilst waiting for a much-relieved driver to reappear.

Most buildings on the island, including the bus shelters, sport roofs of the tiled and pitched variety, which I much prefer to the flat roofed creations on some of the other islands. Pitched roofs mean rain, heavy rain from time to time, but at least it is warm and keeps the island looking fresh and green. Island life is an outdoor one; it is not a shopper's paradise. However, well-stocked Spar grocery stores adorn each village, and there is even an Ikea store to quell any longings for flat pack furniture. The island is well served with accident and emergency centres, together with a well equipped hospital and ambulance service.

Visitors may be accosted by one of the island's 'White Witches'; at least I think they are of the 'White' variety. One appeared at our side whilst we were having a quiet drink in a local bar, and I was struck by the accuracy of her diagnosis and predictions, or was that the gin talking? The bar itself was also a strange phenomena, because as it had many open windows, locals had quickly come to the conclusion that they could avoid the no smoking laws by sitting inside to smoke a cigarette by draping their arm through an open window, and popping their heads outside to take the occasional puff. Legal or not, no one seemed to mind, least of all the police officer chatting to the waitress behind the bar.

Living on a small island of this size certainly has its charms, as well as challenges. This small community is at the mercy of ferries and planes, and travel, despite hefty subsidies, is not cheap. Despite its many attractions, life without many modern conveniences can be hard, particularly for the island's young people trying to achieve a good education and a worthwhile job, as well as for the elderly and infirm. However, experiencing this unique and green paradise, which offers complete silence under a clear night sky, with no light or air pollution, certainly takes some beating.

La Gomera - The Enchanted Island

As part of my on-going love affair with the Canary Islands for my writing, as well as continually updating 'The Canary Islander website', I visit each of the islands regularly. It was recently the turn of La Gomera once again, and although I usually resist naming a favourite island, this must be somewhere at the very top of my list.

La Gomera is an enchanting island. As soon as most people step off the plane, they immediately sense that they are in a very different world from the one that they have left behind. This island is in the form of a volcano, with a World Heritage site, and the Garajonay Forest at its heart. It has towns and villages that fascinate with their beauty and simplicity, as well as beaches of dark sand and a coastline dominated by steep and unyielding cliffs. It is a place where simplicity and peace dominate and there is a sudden rebalancing of harmony with everyday life. For some it may be a shock, and if they want regular transport and a reliable Internet connection, they would be advised to head off to the delights of nearby Tenerife instead!

The cliffs plunge dramatically into the sea, reminding the visitor that this island is the product of many volcanic eruptions, but thankfully not in the last two million years or so. Due to the harsh nature of the landscape, man has only been able to cultivate a small part of it, as seen by the many steep terraces on the mountainsides. As a consequence, over one third of the island's total surface area retains its natural and unspoilt beauty with Garajonay National Park and the

El Cedro Forest being two outstanding examples of their kind.

Many visitors take to the hiking paths and royal roads (caminos reales) in order to get away from the small amount of everyday tourism. If you are fortunate, you can hear examples of the Whistling Language (Silbo), an ancient language that is still used to communicate across the steep ravines that is recognised as culturally significant by UNESCO, and which is the subject of another 'Letter from the Atlantic'.

Wandering in and around the ancient forests quickly became a magical and enchanting experience. I saw insects, birds, plants, trees and shrubs that I have never seen before. It takes time to learn to look, listen, smell and absorb and blend into new surroundings. It was amusing to see, what I refer to as, 'heavy duty' walkers charging down the hiking paths, complete with walking poles, at great speed, determined to complete an impressive number of kilometres that they could brag about over dinner later that evening. Needless to say, most of the group were oblivious to the uniqueness of their surroundings. For me, it was important to allow my senses to slowly absorb my new surroundings and to take over from the usual and mundane for a few days, which became intoxicating and totally relaxing.

There is something unique about this island and as I sat waiting in a newly built, but deserted, airport waiting for my flight home, I wondered for how much longer this island would retain its natural and unique charms set amongst mysterious cliffs, black sand, crystal clear waters and ancient forests. Would this airport soon be alive with dozens of planes arriving from mainland Europe, discharging huge numbers of walking pole carrying passengers, divers and sun seekers? Fingers crossed that they do not stray further across the Atlantic than Tenerife. I will return again very soon.

For photos and more information about this special island, take a look at the 'La Gomera' pages of The Canary Islander website.

Whistling in the Wind

Taking a welcome break during a long walk in a magical wooded valley in the heart of the Garajonay Forest in the small Canary Island of La Gomera, I heard a sound that I had often longed to hear. It was the sound of Silbo Gomera, the whistling language of this unique and beautiful island. This whistling language, the Gomeran whistle, is an ancient local language, which once seemed to be dying out, but is now enjoying something of a revival.

My attention was drawn to a tiny figure further down the valley. The figure was surrounded by what appeared to be goats. As the figure whistled, more goats joined the assembled group. Clearly, the whistling was designed to attract the goats before they moved on. Suddenly, I heard a second whistling sound. This whistle was of a higher pitch, and sounded urgent; it was immediately answered by the first whistle. Sometimes it sounded bird like, with the response more urgent and determined. I sat and listened to what I realised was a fine example of genuine communication between locals, using the whistle language.

Later, I mentioned what I had heard to the barman in the wooden shack that served as a small bar for trekkers. The barman nodded, "Ah yes, that's Santiago with his goats. He lived in Tenerife for a few months to study, but hated the hectic life so much that he returned home to be with his goats. He was training to be a doctor. That's his mother calling him home for lunch, I expect."

Until that moment, I had always thought that the whistle language was something that the locals had reintroduced to keep the tourists on the cruise ships and in restaurants entertained. However, as I spoke to more people on the island, it became clear that the language is very much alive and well, and still used as an effective form of communication.

Experts tell me that the whistle language modifies the Spanish language by replacing it with two whistled vowels and four consonants. The whistle is perfectly suited to the landscape of deep valleys and steep ravines, with the sound travelling up to two miles away. In an area where mobile phone signals are either non-existent, or at best unreliable, I can see its advantages.

Little is known about the origins of the language, other than when the first European settlers arrived in La Gomera during the 15th Century, the locals who were of North African origin, communicated by whistling. When the Spanish invaded, the locals adapted the whistling language to Spanish. It is therefore likely that the whistle originated from African settlers, where there is evidence of other whistled languages used.

Later, a taxi driver recalled the widespread use of the whistle language during troubled times in the 1940s, such as when the mountain caught fire, which it often did. The Guardia Civil would arrive and collect the locals to help put out the fire. Although the council and the mayors were paid to put out the fires, they did not pass on the money to the locals who helped, keeping the money for themselves. In order to avoid the police, the locals would whistle to each other that the police were coming and that they should hide. Members of the Guardia Civil didn't understand whistling and so it was an ideal way of avoiding conscription.

Later, I heard from an old man who told me that learning to whistle wasn't a matter of pleasure or a hobby, but was a social and practical obligation. If you didn't know the language, you would have to walk to give a message, which was not practical in an area of mountains and ravines, and with few roads and no telephones.

In the 1950s, the use of the language began to decline due to economic problems that forced most of the whistlers to emigrate, often to South America or to the larger neighbouring islands. Thanks to European Union funding, the road network was developed, and phones became popular, which made the whistling language almost obsolete.

In the 1990s, there was a major effort to revive the language, which was partly due to making it a compulsory subject in Gomeran primary schools. A few years ago, it used to be true that the language was mostly heard in schools, as well as in restaurants that provide whistling demonstrations for tourists. However, judging from my experiences in the wooded valley, as well as a few days later on a building site where I could hear the same piercing whistle being used by construction workers, I realised that this strange and mystical language has entered a period of serious revival.

For photos and more information about this special island, take a look at the 'La Gomera' pages of The Canary Islander website.

A Live and Let Live Island

The Pride season is once again well under way in many towns and cities across the world, yet for the Canary Islands, Gay Pride is almost over for another year. In May this year, the island of Gran Canaria once again hosted one of the largest Pride events in Europe in Playa del Ingles, Maspalomas, in the south of the island, which it has been doing since 2001. This small island began to heave under the weight of stiletto heels, leathers, feathers and thongs.

As usual, the activities of Maspalomas Gay Pride are focussed in and around the island's Yumbo Centre, which for many has become a kind of 'Gay Heaven' where all manner of people meet and have a thoroughly good time. Its 40 odd bars, discos, saunas, clubs, sex shops and restaurants ensure that there is something for everyone.

I am often asked why this small island, at the very edge of Europe and close to Africa, has become so popular with gay and bisexual men and women, the transgendered, transsexual and the "just confused" from all over the world. Well, there is a story, that I cannot confirm, that back in the 1950s, when Spain was in the grip of the Franco dictatorship, that any military personnel who were found to be gay were shipped off to Spain's penal colony - the island of Gran Canaria, in disgrace and to be forgotten. I guess in many ways, Gran Canaria became Spain's equivalent to Australia, at a time when so many naughty Brits were shipped across to sunnier shores.

Whatever the truth, Gran Canaria now has a well-deserved reputation for its positive 'live and let live' attitudes to life. This is the reason why so many gay men and women fall in love with the island and return year after year, and where many return to live.

Gay Pride has been its usual brash, colourful and non-stop party for the young and not so young. The Parade, which is the highlight of the event, went on for hours, and there are few occasions when so much skin is exposed for such a length of time. Hangovers, sun burn, heat exhaustion came and went, and new relationships began and ended. Pride 2014 was certainly a party to end all parties in the sun.

Next week, we have another Pride celebration in Las Palmas, our capital city in the north of the island. Las Palmas Pride is a much smaller, sober, sensitive and political affair that contrasts well to the non-stop party atmosphere of the much larger event in the south of the island.

Both island events help to remind the world that gay men and women deserve the same rights as others, and people should be free to live their own lifestyle, free of judgement and hate. Pride is a symbol of solidarity and an opportunity to express the vivid personalities that reflect the diverse gay communities throughout the world. Not bad for a small island, is it?

For further information about Maspalomas Gay Pride, do have a look at: www.thegaycanaries.com

Politics

The
Canary
Islander

The Silly Season and the Savage Islands

For those living in Spain, the current diplomatic spats between Spain and the UK about Gibraltar are uncomfortable, and potentially worrying. The previously very good relations between Madrid and London have been overshadowed by a sometimes heated dispute over territory that has lingered for many years. Some reports even claim that the Spanish Foreign Minister recently "hung up" on a telephone call between himself and the UK's Foreign Secretary, William Hague. Many observers claim that the current territorial arguments are due to political and economic tensions in both countries, political and financial scandals in Spain, and embraced in the heady mix of the August 'Silly Season'. Whatever the reasons, frosty relations between countries are unwelcome news for everyone. I can see the argument from both sides, and avoid taking a stance on this particular issue.

Recent news reports of another, and similar dispute, this time between Spain and Portugal, relating to Portugal's Savage Islands, are both interesting and relevant at this particular time. Although vaguely aware of the Savage Islands, I was not aware of any international hostilities until recently. Little public and media attention has been given to this issue, which has troubling international dimensions.

It appears that Spain has quietly lodged an appeal with the United Nations to have the islands, which are Portugal's southernmost territory, reclassified as rocks and not islands. This is not merely a question of semantics, because the main purpose is to reduce

Portugal's exclusive economic zone, which is currently the largest in Europe, and a move that would allow Spanish fishing vessels based in the Canary Islands to fish closer to the Portuguese island of Madeira.

The Savage Islands are located between Spain's Canary Islands and Portugal's Madeira, which allows Portugal's territorial waters to reach within 40 nautical miles of the Spanish territory. In terms of distance, the Savage Islands are closer to the Canary Islands than Madeira. The Savage Islands have been a Portuguese territory since 1438, unlike the Canary Islands that were colonised by the Spanish. Humans had never been known to set foot in the Savage Islands before the Portuguese discovered it. Interestingly, the islands also have a reputation as the treasure islands of pirates, and there are many stories of hunting for treasure. According to a number of documents, serious digs have been attempted in recent years to recover the hidden treasure, but nothing was found.

In more recent times, in 1938, the Permanent Commission of International Maritime Law gave sovereignty of the Savage Islands to Portugal and in 1959, the World Wildlife Fund became interested in the islands and signed a contract with the owner, Luís Rocha Machado. However, in 1971 the Portuguese government intervened and acquired the islands, converting them into a nature reserve.

In 1978, the Savage Islands became part of the Madeira Nature Park, which is one of the oldest nature reserves in Portugal, and in 2002, part of the nature reserve was nominated as a UNESCO World Heritage Site. A small team of wardens currently inhabits the islands. Over the years, the Portuguese navy has seized a number of Spanish fishing vessels for breaching their territorial waters.

In Spain and the Canary Islands, fishermen firmly believe that these islands should be reclassified as rocks. Although the Spanish Government publicly states that they do not have an issue over the sovereignty of the Savage Islands, their reclassification would effectively remove 700 years of Portugal's sovereign rights to the islands.

Portugal is currently responding to Spain's actions with its own submission to the United Nations that contests Spanish claims. In order to underline the point regarding sovereignty, the President of Portugal, Cavaco Silva, recently paid a surprise visit to the islands where he was the first Portuguese head of state to spend a night on the islands, admittedly in the relative comfort of a frigate parked nearby.

The United Nations is expected to issue a verdict on the Savage Islands in 2015. It will be interesting to see if the UN supports the claims of an unpopular Spanish Government towards the Savage Islands, which some claim are similar to the diversionary tactics of the Gibraltar issue. Thank goodness the "Silly Season" is over for another year.

A Cat Among the Canaries

A recent proposal by Spain's Rationalisation of Timetables Association has led the Spanish government in Madrid to debate whether the clocks should be put back an hour to increase productivity and sleeping hours. This suggestion has really put the cat among the Canarians.

The President of the Canarian Government, Paulino Rivero, is very concerned that the islands would "lose their constant mention" in Spain's media if the clocks here were to be the same as the Spanish Peninsular, and lose valuable advertising for the islands in the process. Incidentally, true Canarias never refer to the 'Spanish Mainland' but refer to it as the 'Spanish Peninsular', since real Canarians already regard themselves as being 'on the main land' anyway.

The Canarian President's comments are interesting, because anyone who has switched on Spanish news on the radio or television are likely to be familiar with the phrase "One hour less in the Canaries."

The Canary Islands and their connection with time is a fascinating one, and has an important place in both Canarian and World history; so this is the part where the history and geography lesson begins...

The Greenwich Meridian is an imaginary and arbitrary line that cuts through Spain, UK, France, Algeria and Ghana. It divides the Earth into east and west in much the same way as the Equator divides it into north and south. It enables us to navigate the globe, as well as synchronising the world's clocks. However, this has not always been the case.

Before the important decision around 125 years ago to make Greenwich the centre of world time, many countries and, indeed, large towns kept their own local time. Prior to the important meeting in Washington that took place in 1884 there were, in Europe alone, some 20 different meridians, and you can imagine the confusion.

In AD 127, the Greek astronomer, Ptolemy, selected the Fortunate Islands (the Canaries) as the physical location of the prime meridian when he created an accurate grid system upon which the location of individual cities from the farthest known land west to the farthest known land east could be accurately placed. From that time onwards, early Mediterranean navigators used the meridian through the Canaries, as their first, or prime, meridian as they were then thought to be the most western part of the habitable world.

During the 15th and 16th centuries, when the peoples of Western Europe began to trade by sea, almost every maritime nation used a meridian passing through its own territory as its prime meridian. The French, for instance, used Paris; the Dutch used Amsterdam; and the British used the London meridian. This plethora of prime meridians led to considerable confusion.

The International Meridian Conference of 1884 produced many different views, based upon national self-interest. The final conclusion was to make

Greenwich the standard for setting time with a vote of 22 to one, with only San Domingo voting against and Brazil and France abstaining. France suggested that the new agreed meridian should run through the Canary Islands, which was not French awkwardness, but a suggestion that was soundly based upon the prime meridian as determined by Ptolemy back in AD 127.

Interestingly, Spain moved the clocks forward during the time of the Second World War when the dictator Franco decided to shift to the same time zone as Hitler's Germany. However, in the Canary Islands, the decision was made by King Alfonso XIII in 1922 to be in the same time zone as London. This decision followed pressure from Britain, which had a large commercial trade network in the Canary Islands.

Although the Canary Islands are 2,000 kilometres southwest from Spain's capital, Madrid, the archipelago is currently in the same time zone as London, which is Greenwich Mean Time. However, due to the archipelago's position, the islands should really be one hour behind Greenwich Mean Time, because of its more westerly position in the Atlantic Ocean. It's all a bit of a mess really; however, on some issues, it is better to remain quiet.

ID Cards

Most of those living in Spain are anxious to do their best to fit into their local communities, as well as doing their best to abide by the law. However, sometimes Spain does not make it easy to abide by the law, and the issue that I raise here is a good example.

How many in Spain remember that rather useful identification card that was awarded to those who could meet the residency requirements a few years ago? This credit card size piece of identification not only carried the all-important identification number and fingerprint, but a photo as well, which meant that it could be used for identification purposes in shops, banks, dealing with the authorities, as well as internal flights.

Sadly, someone complained bitterly that an ID card was an insult to the status of being a European citizen, and it should not be necessary. Sadly, he was taken seriously, and the implications were insufficiently considered. The fact that most European countries have their own system of ID cards was overlooked, and so the decision in Madrid to cancel ID cards for all foreigners was no big deal, because those from other European countries could manage quite well with the ones issued by their own governments, although still lacking the Spanish ID number.

Not so in the UK. No doubt many will remember the furore that the possible introduction of National Identity Cards in the UK caused. There was a predictable response about human rights and personal freedom in the press, which meant that the UK government could not proceed with the planned introduction to bring the UK in line with the rest of Europe, and the project was scrapped

To the irritation of many British residents in Spain, who were now left without any form of national identification, other than an A4 green sheet of paper issued by the Spanish authorities, this turnaround was nothing short of a disaster. The new form of identification did not contain a passport photo, which meant that a passport has, in theory, to be made available at all times, as it is the only valid and recognised form of identification that Brits have. Passports and UK driving licences do not carry the all important Spanish national identification number, and so the A4 green paper has to be carried as well. The authorities are also quite strict in insisting that the original A4 green sheet of paper be used and that copies are not acceptable. You can imagine the state of some of these flimsy and well-worn documents. A credit card sized version of the document was made available by the authorities in 2012, but was of little use since it still did not include a photo.

Many have tried to get around the issue by continuing to use a laminated version of their old ID card, which is against the law and can lead to a hefty fine. In my own case, I photocopied the A4 green sheet of paper, together with my passport, which I had validated by a notary, as well as the police. Both have been rejected on several occasions, with the authorities insisting on seeing the original documents. Most that I know now tend to use their UK driving licence, if they still have one, in conjunction with A4 green sheet of paper, but there remains a strong likelihood of the document being rejected by an over zealous 'jobsworth' without an accompanying passport.

It now seems that all is about to change with the reintroduction of the ID card. This is an initiative that has been spearheaded by a group in the Balearic Islands who made representations to the EU, as well as to Members of Parliament in Madrid. The matter is now in the hands of the Head of Police and the Secretary of State who are studying the issue. It seems that something is moving, but as yet no there is formal confirmation or announcement.

For fear that this could be yet another case of 'bar room gossip', I checked the information with the British Embassy in Madrid, who have issued the following statement, albeit in Diplomatic Non-Speak:

"All EU citizens planning to reside in Spain for more than three months should register in person at the Oficina de Extranjeros in their province of residence or at designated Police stations. They will then be issued with a Residence Certificate stating their name, address, nationality, NIE number (Número de Identificación Extranjeros) and date of registration.

"We are aware of a campaign by some EU citizens resident in Spain to seek changes in the format of the Residence Certificate. Ultimately it is a matter for the Spanish authorities to decide."

Although the timescale is uncertain, it does seem that something is happening at last, and it should become a little easier to abide by the law.

Be Careful Of What We Wish For

The whole concept of 'Brits in Europe' is a controversial area that I know many living in Spain get very heated about. Indeed, it is one subject that is a hot topic of conversation in many Brit bars and gatherings. However, it is also fair to say that many really don't care at all about the issue, and have no interest in voting in the forthcoming European Elections.

I care passionately about the whole idea of being a European. For many years, I have regarded myself firstly as a European, secondly, as British and thirdly as an Englishman. For me, it is one of the best things that has happened, both politically and culturally, during my lifetime. From the moment that Britain joined Europe it meant that any European could live and work in any other European country as equals; well, that's the theory, although we all know that there can be variations in this interpretation.

I fervently hope that Britain stays within the European family if there is ever a referendum on the issue. Personally, I would hate Britain to be on the outside and looking in with no influence about what is happening in Europe, but feeling the impact of any decisions made. Many of our European friends, the Germans, French and Spanish in particular, are bewildered by Britain's lukewarm attitudes to Europe.

It is true that Spanish attitudes towards Europe are changing from one of blind acceptance and trust to a healthier one that is beginning to question and challenge some of the more obscure rules that appear from Brussels from time to time. Even so, the bond is strong and it would be unusual to visit any official building, building development or project without seeing three flags flying: the Canarian and Spanish flags flying alongside that of the European Union. Compare that with the UK where seeing the EU flag flying anywhere is unusual.

Britain has always been an awkward partner, made worse by the years of recession. As history teaches us, during periods of economic downturn, there is a tendency to look for scapegoats, be it the treatment of Jews, gays and travellers in Germany during the Second World War to the Poles, Bulgarians and Lithuanians in the UK in current times. It is a human reaction to group together and to blame someone or something else, even if it defies logic. It is also worth noting that many observers, and particularly those from the US, see Britain as currently being in a highly beneficial and unique position within Europe; remaining outside the Eurozone and retaining its own currency.

I often despair of bar room discussions from those who vehemently demonstrate their hatred of all things European and even their host country, which in the main has welcomed them so warmly. It is not that long ago when some of our friends needed a work permit to work in Spain, so that they were unable to purchase property or to start their own businesses until Britain became a member of the EU. One can only imagine what would happen if Britain did eventually pull out of Europe. The signs are already that the barriers to free movement would once again reappear and that Britain would be isolated from its European counterparts in many ways.

The British Government's political yet popular decisions to restrict immigration, and use of the health service and benefits to migrants from European countries are already beginning to show as retaliatory moves against British residents in some countries. I often hear of their problems with health, unemployment, pensions and social benefits that were unknown a short time ago. Health services, in particular, have been severely curtailed in some countries, including Spain, in recent months.

The global recession, as well as a less welcoming policy towards foreigners, has led to less flexibility and generosity towards them than have been experienced in the past. Politicians need to be fully aware that actions taken in Britain are reflected in other member states, and it is British people living in Europe who suffer the often-unintended consequences. Let us be careful of what we wish and vote for.

Europe

I usually try to avoid political issues, but many residents have shared with me their concerns about the recent European Elections. Apathy, as well as dissatisfaction with much of Europe's political system and political classes, seems to be at the root of the problem. Even so, voting in the European Elections is the only opportunity that we, as foreigners, get to express our feelings yet, sadly, many that I know could not even be bothered to put down their gin and tonics for a few minutes and toddle off to their nearest polling station.

I watched the results of the UK local and European elections with dismay. Those living in the UK know more about UKIP than I, and will be better placed to make more informed judgments. I am concerned about the implications of UKIP's success, as well as their growing influence upon the UK political landscape, for both current as well as those hoping to live and work in Europe.

Despite the views of its critics, the right to live and work in any country in the EU is a wonderful thing, which should not be given up lightly. There are currently over 300,000 retired British people living in Europe, and many of whom seem to be oblivious to what the UK's potential withdrawal from the EU could mean for them. Experts agree that pensions, health benefits and investments would all be under threat should the UK withdraw from the European Union.

It is quite clear that UK residents currently have very little representation in the UK. It also appears that there are only very few British politicians who are concerned about the welfare of UK nationals living and working overseas. However, we must remember that we can only live in the country of our choice at the whim of politicians, in agreement with the EU. Should the UKIP bandwagon advance yet further, it could force a referendum that leads to a UK exit from Europe, which could spell disaster for all British people living in Europe.

We are often told that one of the reasons for the rise of UKIP is the disenchantment of voters with the number of immigrants, European and others, entering the UK. Surely, this argument could also refer to the people of Spain, Italy and France with regard to British people? I am well aware of the cultural changes that a large number of Brits, for instance, bring to a Spanish village or small town. Is it not reasonable to assume that there could be resentment in much the same way towards us, and particularly if the UK is no longer part of the European family?

To spell it out more clearly, if the UK leaves Europe, it would mean that we would cease to be European citizens and we could no longer have the right to live and move freely in Europe. European laws would no longer protect us, and the right to ensure that British State pensions would be paid in full in Europe would cease. Other benefits would cease to be protected too, including reciprocal health care arrangements that are so important for the retired residents. We would be living in a foreign state, just as any other country outside the EU. In short, should a referendum take place, there is a strong possibility that our lives would change considerably, and not for the better.

The cynics will raise the issue of Switzerland and other countries that, although not part of the European Union, have negotiated agreements and exemptions in favour of their citizens living in other European countries. They argue that no doubt the same would apply to the UK, should an exit occur. It may be the case, but it may not. Personally, I prefer to have the reassurance of a system, as imperfect as it may be, that guarantees me the right to live elsewhere in Europe, and not be at the mercy of populist governments and political parties of the day.

Statistics and Sunshine

I rarely trust statistics, and particularly those in articles in the press that begin with "According to the latest statistics...". I know far too much about how 'flexible' statistics can be, and how they can be twisted and manipulated to match the political arguments and headline grabbing deceptions of the day.

Recent headlines in the UK press screaming "One in five British Expats in Spain returning home" and "End to the Mediterranean Dream for British Expats", and "Has the Sun Set on the Expat Dream in Spain?" caught my attention recently. They were an amusing read, but I felt that they required rather more clarification.

Distrustful as I am of UK statistics, I am equally cynical about Spanish data. In the case of Brits returning home, the statistics came directly from Spanish Town Halls, which are not exactly renowned as being at the pinnacle of statistical efficiency. This data comes, of course, from British residents taking the trouble to register with the authorities and entering their names on the register; many do not, and particularly those who have holiday or rental homes, and intend to live in Spain for less than six months each year.

Back to the headline grabbing horrors, "One in five British expats in Spain returning home". What the article doesn't mention, of course, is that four out of every five residents still choose to live in Spain, and are very happy about it. This is merely a different interpretation of the same set of statistics, but it doesn't make such a good headline, does it?

It is true, of course, that the recession and reduction in job opportunities have led to serious financial difficulties for many who have decided to return to their countries of origin. However, suggestions that sun seeking retired people now prefer to give up on the traditional retirement hotspots of Spain, France and Portugal in order to live in Dubai, the Caribbean, Thailand or even Switzerland are simply ridiculous.

Since I moved to Spain, there has always been movement of those who longed for a new life in the sun, only to find that it was not for them. Many were unwilling or unable to learn the language, appreciate the culture, missed British TV, or continually complained about an exchange rate that was lower than expected. These people quickly returned to their home countries, realising that life abroad was not for them. Others faced the hardships of death of a partner, family problems, serious illness or breakdown in relationships, making a return to the UK inevitable.

Statistics aside, my own contacts in the removals business in the Costa Blanca, Costa del Sol and the Canary Islands confirm that there is by no means a one-way exodus to the UK. Retired people, seeing the property bargains to be had in Spain, France and Portugal are heading out to pick up a dream property at a good price. Prices in favourite retirement destinations, such as the Balearics and the Canary Islands, remain buoyant, because of considerable interest from Scandinavian, German, Russian and even Chinese buyers.

I also know of many who have returned to the UK, mainly for financial or health reasons. In many cases, those who have returned have not settled well in their home country, and their one aim is to return to Spain at the earliest possible opportunity, and when their personal circumstances improve.

So, for those who have deserted a gentler and more relaxed life in the sun to return to the cold, damp UK, I raise a glass and wish you well. However, the use of flawed statistics by the press do not tell the true story, which is that most of us are very content with our lives in the sun!

Bugs and Beasties

The
Canary
Islander

The Super Cockroach

I have a great respect for cockroaches. I am not saying that I would want one as a pet, but I do respect them, as well as for their ability to survive in the most unlikely of conditions and treatment by humans. I certainly agree with the view that if, or when, the World is decimated by nuclear disaster, cockroaches will live on.

I remember writing a series of articles about cockroaches for a newspaper several years ago. It covered all facets of these fascinating creatures, including how tasty they can be if fried. Sadly, I received a few letters of complaint, as well as quite a few from interested chefs, so I will not go into too much detail here for fear of upsetting the delicate stomach once again.

My eye was drawn to a recent article about a species of cockroach that has recently invaded New York. Apparently these invaders are a species previously unseen in the US, which can withstand the harsh winter cold, as well as freezing conditions. This new and rather entertaining species, commonly known as Periplanetea Japonica (a name that sounds rather nice and floral) is quite common in Asia, but unseen in the US until recently. It is assumed that a few stowaways may have arrived in the US as illegal immigrants by stowing away in a few pot plants. Ingenious little things, aren't they?

Sadly, the home species of cockroach in the US are less than happy, because the invaders will compete for their food, as well as space. Fortunately, experts predict that this will mean that the illegal immigrants will spend so much time in competing it will mean that they will have less energy to reproduce. Hmm, maybe these experts should think again. I am no expert, but I can think of many examples of other species, including the human race, whereby the breeding instinct becomes even stronger during difficult conditions, such as in the UK during particularly cold weather or in war torn areas of the world. The inclination to breed and to replace itself is an instinct that US biologists seem to have forgotten.

In any case, and on a more practical note, the biologists are quite sure that the new species will not breed with the local population and create some kind of 'super species' because 'their genitalia fit together like a lock and key' within the same species. The experts are so confident about this one that they explain it as being rather like fitting a Yale key into a Chubb lock, but I won't go into detail. In any case, I am not convinced that they are right on this one either.

I remember that a few years ago when I was taking my dog, Bella, for a short walk, the entire road was covered with an army of many thousands of cockroaches. I have never seen so many gathered together in one place, and it was just like an invasion. I am told that they appear from their hiding places at times of crisis, such as during periods of intense heat or flood. It was a particularly hot day and I guess they had all popped out for a spot of sun bathing. However, it was not such a good idea, because the sound of crunching that could be heard as vehicles swept by and skidded over them was not pleasant, although a few minutes later they had all disappeared. Bella, who is not the bravest dog on the island, was terrified, and so we headed home rather more quickly than usual. Yes, I really do think that cockroaches will one day rule the world.

Laundry Tips

Sorry about the title, but after several weeks writing about Wills, Death and Cockroaches, I thought it was time to move on to something a little more cheerful, and that this would catch your attention. Let us consider a subject that I know is very dear to the hearts of many, and that is the subject of washing clothes.

Long gone are the days when most would pop along to their local stream and give their clothes a good scrub in its cooling running water. Believe it or not, the question of washing is one of the subjects that I receive many questions about. True, it is a little behind the usual questions about 'the land grab', legal and motoring problems, but washing is a popular subject nevertheless. It seems that sometimes we are never happy. We spend much of our lives in the misery of living in the wind and rain in our home country, move to Spain and still complain about the weather, but this time about what it does to the laundry.

The problem is that although clothes dry very rapidly in the heat of the Spanish and Canarian sun, they dry a little too quickly for comfort and end up feeling like sandpaper. We can add as much fabric conditioner as we wish, but it makes little difference. Just imagine the horrors of enjoying your time swimming, sunbathing and relaxing in the heat of the sun on one of our fabulous beaches, only to take a delicious shower at the end of it all and dry yourself off with a towel that feels at best like a sheet of limp cardboard or, at worst, a nasty Brillo pad! Not nice is it?

133

Now, thanks to many who write to me, I think we have the answer. It does not come cheap, but it is the answer nevertheless, and it comes in the form of a tumble drier. I can already hear some readers snorting in disgust at the very thought of living in a hot climate and using a tumble drier to dry the washing, but I can assure them that after thorough testing, the idea does work. First of all, washing enthusiasts can still dry their clothes and towels in the heat of the sun, in the usual way. This is economically and environmentally essential; after all we don't want to increase our carbon footprint more than we have already. However, for the final ten to fifteen minutes of drying, just pop the towels into the tumble drier to finish off. They will come out of the machine warm, dry and, most importantly, soft and fluffy; just like the towels that mother gave you at home.

Incidentally, whilst on the subject of fabric conditioners, it is best not to use them at all. I had not realised until a correspondent wrote to me recently that most fabric conditioners are made from the products of the slaughterhouse, and with animal fats being one of the main ingredients. In addition, although fabric conditioners may make your clothes feel soft and fresh, the chemicals used are also toxic. Health problems can range from headaches, light headedness and fatigue to serious damage to organs and the central nervous system, as well as cancer. I had always thought that the 'fresh clean' smell of 'Spring Blossom' fabric conditioner was for my sensory benefit. Apparently not, as it is there mainly to disguise the foul smelling chemicals used. I am told that, as an alternative, a quarter cup of white vinegar or baking soda can be used in the final wash instead. To end on a more cheerful note, that 'heady feel' after a good night out may have nothing at all to do with too much alcohol, but might be the result of contact with just too much fabric conditioner.

A Good Deed for the Day

After a short lived affair as a cub scout, where I learned to leap out of trees badly, build shelters that collapsed and was never able to light fires by rubbing stones (or was it sticks?) together, as well an assortment of valuable life saving skills. I also learned to be kind and helpful to retired and elderly peoplc; to my young mind, apparently, they liked nothing more than being helped across the road, whether or not they wanted to go. However, I did disappointingly notice that retired folk tended to be a bit mean during those exciting 'Bob a Job' weeks', which thankfully were banned some years ago, being considered as gross exploitation of seven-year-olds. After all, a 'bob', which is now five pence in modern money, wasn't really an attractive rate of pay for helping to paint a living room or dig an allotment. All those distant, and mostly fond, memories came flooding back to me this week after an unfortunate incident at the rubbish bins.

I was taking our dog, Bella, for her morning walk, when I thought I would walk via the village rubbish bins with a bag of rubbish. Unlike better organised municipalities on the island, which have smart stainless steel hoppers leading to cavernous bins set well below street level, our municipality, which tends to have only an interest in the more prosperous tourist areas, provides smelly open-topped hoppers where all manner of vermin congregate, as well as a unhealthy gang of people searching through the rubbish trying to find something that they can sell. Times are hard for some people, and I can understand why they do this, but it often leads to arguments and fights, as to who found something of value first. It is a place where Bella and I do not linger for long.

I strode over to the bin and threw in my bag of rubbish. It was then that I noticed a small, elderly lady trying to throw a small carrier bag of rubbish into the hopper, which was far too high for her to reach. She was clearly arthritic, and her weak throw meant that her carrier bag fell well short of its target. I picked up her bag and threw it in for her. The elderly lady smiled gratefully and mumbled a 'Gracias' and then added something else, which I could not fully understand. I then noticed a second carrier bag in her other hand.

I smiled and grabbed the bag from her hand, although I noticed that she did seem to be holding it rather tightly. This time, the old lady looked at me, shook her head and mumbled something in bad Spanish, which I took to be "I can manage". My cub scout training certainly would not let me take no for an answer when there was an elderly person in need, and so I replied with a smile, adding "De nada" (which loosely translated means "it is nothing"), tossed the second carrier bag into the bin and went on my way, feeling satisfied that I had done my bit to help an elderly person in distress. Akela would be pleased with me.

Bella was anxious to continue with her walk and dragged me across the road aiming for the place where she usually likes to run and search for lizards. As I walked passed the hoppers, I noticed the old lady still standing by the bins, pointing and shouting at where I had thrown her carrier bag. I paused as I noticed that someone had climbed into the hopper, retrieved the elderly lady's second carrier bag and was passing it to her. The dreadful truth slowly dawned on me. I had not only retrieved and thrown the lady's first carrier bag of rubbish into the hopper, but I had also grabbed her second carrier bag, which probably contained groceries, into the hopper too.

I felt both guilt and acute embarrassment as I walked quickly away from the scene, but pleased that the elderly lady was now reunited with her groceries, whilst no doubt complaining about the thoughtless Brit who had thrown her shopping into the bin.

I blame it all on the cub scouts. Although I meant well, next time I will curb my enthusiasm to be helpful to elderly people who seem to be in need.

Paparazzi

A few days ago I received an email from what I had previously thought was a reputable media agency in New York, asking me if I knew of a good "paparazzi style" photographer on the island or, failing that, would I be prepared to "do the job"? Apparently, there was a Very Important Person on the island, and the magazine wanted to obtain a collection of photos for their publications, as well as providing material for others who were interested.

Our islands regularly welcome a fair number of the famous, rich and powerful and well-heeled members of society. We are used to accommodating film stars, rappers, royals and politicians, corrupt or otherwise. We often see them out and about, in bars, restaurants or local shops. Indeed, I had a brief chat with one celebrity, who will remain nameless, over the cheese counter at Carrefour only last week. It was good to see him looking so relaxed, and he appeared so much smaller, as well as better presented, in real life than he does on the TV screen. I did not ask for an autograph, but merely suggested that he ask the assistant for a piece of the cheese to sample before purchase. He seemed grateful for my suggestion.

Most of the better hotels and restaurants on the islands appreciate the privacy and discretion that their more famous clients expect; sensibly recognising that it is essential for future recommendations and business. There are exceptions, of course, but it is rare. It is quite simple; those businesses that are not discrete simply lose business, and word gets around fast on an island.

Maybe we are being spoilsports for not joining in with the fun. After all, just a few photos with a long lens of a beautiful girl or a good looking guy sunbathing on one of our beautiful beaches would provide some titivation and entertainment on a wet, cold Sunday morning for readers in the UK or US. Surely there is no harm in a little of that? Actually there is, and many see the behaviour of those engaged in paparazzi style activities as akin to stalking, taking advantage and invading personal space.

In many countries, anti-stalking laws are rightly in place to protect the lives of public figures and celebrities. As we have heard in the lengthy phone hacking trials in the UK, the courts agree that everyone is entitled to some degree of privacy in their lives, and the general public is beginning to recognise that there is a line, albeit a fine one, to be drawn between private and public lives. Our lives are not an open book for everyone to read, and some degree of privacy should be guaranteed.

Yes, I do know several excellent and more than capable photographers on the island, but I certainly would not suggest any for paparazzi work attempting to embarrass the rich, famous, powerful or just very fortunate on holiday. Those that I know would not want the job anyway.

The 'Can't Do' Bureaucrat

I hate wasting time, and Spanish bureaucracy is one of the greediest when it comes to pointless time wasting activities. In my experience, the bureaucrats of all nations are two distinct species, the ones who 'can do' and the ones who 'can't do' – in other words, jobsworths. This more depressing of the species is also part of the 'my glass is half empty' rather than the more positive 'my glass is half full' bureaucrat.

Mobile phone networks are one of the few things that I dislike about life in Spain. By all accounts, this view is not restricted to Spain, but is a common criticism of phone companies in other countries too. During the years that I have lived in Spain, I have tried all the networks and each time have suffered poor quality service, high pricing, together with a 'couldn't care less' attitude to customer service. The fun and games often plummet to new lows when it comes to the termination of a mobile phone contract. Several years ago, it took me six months to terminate a contract that had already ended.

I promised that I would never again be caught by a mobile phone contract in Spain. As a result, I usually purchase an unlocked mobile phone in the UK and use it with a prepaid Spanish sim card. Several years ago, a good friend advised me to try a new company that offered fair pricing, good coverage and a no nonsense approach to its business. I have been with them since the service began, albeit by obtaining a card from my friend living in the Peninsular, as the service was not, until recently, available in the Canary Islands.

A smart new 4G phone, together with 4G coverage in my area, means that I have been finally tempted away in favour of another company, since my current company is unlikely to offer a 4G service for some time. However, before I can access the delights of 4G, I have to have a contract, without a new phone, with the company as part of the deal. I decided to forget my earlier promise, and headed off to the nearest shop to sign up and collect the new sim card for my phone.

Knowing how Spanish bureaucrats have an unhealthy greed for all paperwork, I took my residency document, national identity number, copy of my passport (notarised by the police and a notary), bank details, utility bills, together with details of my existing phone service to the mobile phone shop.

The unhelpful and miserable looking man at the counter, a 'can't do bureaucrat' if ever there was one, took a cursory look at my documents, sniffed and muttered that I needed to get a copy of a paid utility bill from my bank before he could give me a sim card. I headed off to the bank, queued for the obligatory 90 minutes, and was eventually issued with what I was told was the correct document, which would satisfy any mobile phone company.

I headed back to the phone shop and cheerfully presented the document. Again, the 'can't do bureaucrat' took a brief glance at the piece of paper, shook his head and said that it had to be officially stamped by the bank, which it was not. I drove back to the bank, where I adopted the Canarian technique of importantly moving to the front of the queue with a

"Will you just?" question. No one appeared to mind too much, my document was stamped, signed and dated and I headed back to the shop.

The 'can't do bureaucrat' examined my documents, smirked, shook his head and told me that I needed to bring my original passport to the shop. Now, I have been caught by this one many times before and since being robbed and relieved of my passport in Madrid many years ago, my passport is securely locked away and never sees the light of day until I leave the island. I use a notarised and police verified document, which is always accepted without question. However, this time was to be the exception.

With my patience now stretched to the limit, I returned to the shop with the original documents. The 'can't do bureaucrat' examined all the documents once again, gave a brief nod, but then told me that he didn't have the very small nano sim cards in stock and that I would have to wait for a few days until they arrived from Barcelona and return to the shop to collect the card. I collected my documents, told the 'can't do bureaucrat' to forget it, returned home and completed the entire transaction on line in a few minutes. The sim card arrived by courier two days later.

This entire experience took the best part of a day and once again reminded me of the horrors of mobile phone contracts, as well as how easy it is to fall into a Spanish bureaucratic nightmare. My best advice is to stick with a prepaid sim, or if you must have a contract and are computer and Spanish language savvy, do it yourself on line.

The Stuff of Life

Who am I to judge?

These five words are perhaps the five most powerful and significant words spoken by Pope Francis since he became leader of the Catholic Church. Although I am not a Catholic, I do not automatically respect the leader of any Church or organisation, unless they have earned it through not only their words but, most importantly, their actions. However, these words spoken whilst addressing the issue of gay men and women in the Church did make me sit up and listen.

Judging others is perhaps one of the easiest and most destructive things that people indulge in. Many write to tell me of their damaging experiences with other people when arriving in their new country. They arrive full of anticipation and hope for a new life in their chosen country, only to be met by cynicism and suspicion from the 'established' residents living in their communities. Many tell me of the 'pecking order' that has quickly established itself in the ghettos of the Costas. Instead of a warm welcome, many tell me that they witness a degree of hostility upon their arrival. A seemingly innocent welcome drink with the neighbours is often followed by a barrage of questions designed to draw out the personal circumstances, fortunes and health of the newcomer.

Of course, psychologists will tell us that this destructive inquisitiveness is a way that current residents defend their existing, and often hard won, territories, image and position in the community. As with any animal grouping, these people fiercely defend their rights against a possible intruder should they feel threatened in any way. All communities quickly develop spokesmen and leaders within their community. Often this is a good thing, but only if fulfilled with humility and tolerance.

I recall one self-appointed spokesman for a newly built block of apartments that we were living in when we first moved to Spain. Each block of apartments should have a 'Community', which is a legal entity designed to govern and oversee the maintenance, cleanliness of the shared areas, as well as the rights of owners of the apartments. In our case, this did not happen, and a forthright and outspoken German lady stepped in to fulfil this role. During some of those dreadful days when the lift was not working, the electricity and water was disconnected and repairs were needed, this community spirited lady took on the fight with builders, the Town Hall, water and electricity companies. She bullied, argued and cajoled to do what was right for all of the residents living in the apartment. In the end, she won and we were all exceedingly grateful to her.

I contrast this to another case that I have recently heard of, whereby a long-term British woman, married to a Spanish man, maliciously gossiped about her neighbours, whom she did not like, and claimed that they were responsible for a number of local burglaries. She had no evidence, but the seed of doubt that she planted into the minds of some created a situation whereby she skilfully began to turn the entire street against one particular family, whom she did not approve of, and had a personal vendetta against. Quite simply, neighbours believed what she said simply because she had lived in Spain for many years and could speak the language fluently. She felt that this distinction gave her the right to be appointed as sole judge and jury. More astute neighbours began to ask questions, but the damage had already been done, because the seed of doubt had been sown.

All communities can become potentially destructive, and this community is no different to any other. Lack of understanding of language and culture, as well as undeserved respect for those that have been in the country longer may make the newcomer complacent as to what is right and what is wrong. It is important that all residents retain an open mind, determine what is right and wrong for themselves, and not be easily influenced by established residents who see themselves as top of the 'pecking order'.

'Who am I to judge?' asked the Pope. For once, I agree wholeheartedly with him.

Where there's a Will...

Several of our friends have died this year. It comes to us all eventually; death, that is. As the old adage goes, 'the two certainties in life are death and taxation', and the death of family and close friends certainly concentrates the mind. Without being too morbid about the issue, I guess the only way to deal with it, as it is a certainty, is that we had better ensure that we make a good job of it, and not create too much of a burden for others after our passing.

A few days ago, I received an email from a recently retired British couple, who had moved to Spain and needed a will to cover their new property. They asked if they could simply update their UK wills, or whether they need to have new ones prepared especially for their new assets in Spain?

There seems to be considerable uncertainty amongst many, who think that as they have a will in the UK, there is no need to have one in Spain. I still even meet those who boast over their gin and tonics that they have no written wills at all, and that Spanish inheritance laws will deal nicely with the issue when the time comes. Maybe this is the case, but only after considerable expense and distress for those that they leave behind.

This often-held view about inheritance laws may be partly true if the transfer of the estate is a simple one; for example, from husband to wife. However, it is not without considerable expense and delays for heirs if there is no Spanish will and executors have to rely on a UK will. The reason is that Spanish inheritance laws are very different from those in the UK, and that there is no guarantee that assets will be distributed in the way that the deceased had intended.

The message is clear; it is important that those with property or other assets in the country make a Spanish will. Having a Spanish will does not mean that your UK will is forgotten. However, your UK will would be concerned only with those assets that you still own in the UK, whilst your Spanish will would deal with your Spanish property and assets. Needless to say, it is very important that you continue to update both wills should circumstances change, such as separation, divorce or death of a partner.

It is important to remember that if an update to your UK will is required, your Spanish will is not revoked in the process. The best way to overcome this issue is to ensure that the first clause of your UK will has words to the effect of "I revoke all my earlier UK Wills, but not my Spanish Will", or words to that effect.

In Spain, there are many people who will offer to prepare your Spanish will for you. Be careful with this one; my best advice is to have it prepared by a suitably qualified Spanish lawyer, and registered at the Central Wills Registry in Madrid.

Abandoned

When planning a new life abroad, many forget to seriously consider the implications of disability, advancing age, serious illness and death of a partner later in their lives. These are all issues that readers often tell me about and many realise too late that their new life in the sun has turned into a living nightmare.

One of the issues is due to cultural differences; for example, in most Mediterranean countries, it is the cultural norm for the old and sick to be cared for by their own family members, unlike in the UK and Scandinavia, where many of the elderly spend the latter stages of their lives in sheltered accommodation or in residential care. As a result, there are few residential homes available in countries such as Spain and Portugal, and sudden illness and changes in other circumstances may mean that it is too late to return to the UK for the necessary care.

End of life care is also another area to consider, since many countries are unable to offer the comprehensive range of services and support that are available in the UK. For instance, in the Canary Islands, there are no hospices or Macmillan nurses to care for the dying.

I recall one very sad case from the Costa Blanca, where one British family abandoned their elderly mother in a local hospital, because they claimed that they could no longer cope with her. The old lady was living in a retirement home in the UK before her son took her to Spain in a bid to save the remaining part of the family estate from the cost of residential care. After a few months in Spain, the old lady was abandoned at a local hospital. On arrival at hospital she was found to be dehydrated, malnourished, yet fully aware of what was going on, as she had no serious health problems. The elderly woman was discharged from the hospital five days later and an ambulance returned her to her son's home. The son wanted nothing more to do with her and sent her back to the hospital.

The hospital returned the old lady to her son's home a second time, but this time accompanied by the police, who handed the son a denuncia (a police report), but the son still refused to accept any responsibility for her. The son was then summoned to court, for which he failed to appear and subsequently he left the area with his family, but without his mother and could not be traced. The old lady, although mentally sound, had a stomach condition and could not live alone as she required a strict diet and regular, supervised medication.

It was left to the courts to decide what to do with the old lady, with the option of either placing her into one of the few care homes in the Costa Blanca, at the expense of the State, or returning her to the UK where she would be with people who could speak the same language.

Although hard to believe, I understand that hospitals report that this situation is becoming quite common and worsens during holiday periods. We often hear of heart-breaking stories of dogs being abandoned during the summer holidays, but abandoning an elderly person overseas takes cruelty to an entirely new level.

The Stuff of Nightmares

The World recession has had many unexpected and sad consequences, some of which will remain with us for many years to come. Unemployment, poverty and home repossessions are all topics that we are familiar with. However, it seems that the dead also have not escaped the ravages of the recession.

In Spain, as in many other countries, there are facilities for leaving one's body to medical science upon death. Some may wish to leave their bodies to enable their organs to be used for transplant purposes, others may wish to donate their body to medical science for use by medical students, as well as furthering the cause of conquering many diseases. Both intentions should be applauded, and is an option than many retired people may consider.

Sadly, due to the high cost of funerals, the option of leaving bodies to medical science has increased in recent years, and particularly following the recession. I know of a number of retired people who have done this in order for those left behind to escape funeral costs when the time comes. Like many people, I had always assumed that when the medical institution finished with the body, there is a simple funeral and it is cremated in a dignified way, and paid for by the receiving institution. Apparently, this is not the case.

A major Spanish newspaper has recently discovered hundreds of dead bodies, originally donated to science, that have been left at room temperature in the basement of a Spanish university for many years. In the basement of one Madrid University are an estimated 250 corpses, which are leftovers from students' experiments.

The newspaper described it as "the stuff of nightmares", a genuine chamber of horrors, publishing photographs that displayed lines of "mummified" corpses lined up on a shelf. Staff at the university commented that the arrangements were in order, although admitted that some of the bodies had been stored for "up to five years."

Apparently, the member of staff who operated the incinerating oven took early retirement and the university was unable to advertise the position, because the unions said that the oven was in a poor condition and emitted poisonous gases. Later, the university commented that a solution had been found, and that a funeral company would start removing the bodily remains.

Although the Spanish Anatomy Society has guidelines on the storage of bodies donated to science, there is no formal legal framework. Spain's Health Department commented that its laws only dealt with burials, autopsies and the transfer of bodies, while the Education Department said universities were independent institutions outside of their control.

The university receives more than fifty bodies each year as more people donate their bodies to medical science as a way of avoiding funeral costs. However, the donors and their families are unclear what happens to the bodies once they are of no further use. This is certainly an area that residents should clarify before considering donations to medical science, together with under what circumstances the body could be refused when death occurs, leaving families with unintended and unexpected funeral costs.

The Last Gin and Tonic

So, what do you want done with your body when you have finally drunk your last gin and tonic? Yes, I know that this is not the cheeriest subject to read, but it must be said, and the issue has to be faced. This is an area that few wish to consider, and recent personal experiences have alerted me to some of the dangers of ignoring the issue.

I have to admit that this is not an area that I have given too much thought too either. Burial and cremation sound rather old hat, burial at sea rather more romantic, but I am not a good sailor. Then there is embalming; I rather fancied being pickled in a very large vat of fine malt, but one of my friends thought it would be a waste of good malt.

For foreign residents, the choices are rather limited. The obvious choice is, of course, cremation. It is quickly done and dusted, if you forgive the pun, and then your loved ones can scatter your ashes in a favourite place, or, after quite a lot of bureaucracy and additional expense, you can be popped into a special container, flown home in style, preferably not by a certain low cost Irish airline, and scattered lovingly somewhere in the country from where you tried so desperately hard to escape.

There is burial of course, but in many countries, this is not burial in a green and pleasant churchyard, which appeals to many, flooding aside. In many countries, 'burial' means merely being popped into a kind of filing cabinet for the length of time that has been paid for. So what happens after expiry of the 25

---

or 50 years that the inheritors of your estate have begrudgingly paid for? Yes, you guessed it, out you come! I leave the rest to your imagination.

Then there is the option of leaving your body to medical science. This could be either for transplanting various bits and pieces to people who really need it, which would be very useful. Alternatively, your body could go for medical science and be used by student medics to examine various body parts and tissues. Now, I am not that altruistic, and personally I find this all rather distasteful. However, I know that many, and particularly those who have been in the medical profession, find this idea appealing. Should this be the case, I urge intending donors to carefully check out all the facts before registration and to read the small print about the medical institution's right to refuse your body when the time comes. Sometimes, it may be that, in cases such as cancer, they do not wish to have the body, or simply that they have too many.

One forgotten impact of the financial crisis is that there are often more donations of bodies for medical research than are needed in some countries. Quite simply, donors sometimes donate their bodies to escape high funeral costs, as the receiving institution usually pays for the final disposal of the body. In turn, this has meant that there is often a surplus of bodies and an intended well-meaning donation is refused when the time comes. This can cause enormous unexpected financial problems and distress for the families of the departed.

Funeral costs are very high in many countries, and it is wise to take out a funeral plan to pay for these costs. Premiums are usually very reasonable, and the earlier such a policy is started the cheaper the premiums will be. When the time comes, the existence of a funeral plan can take away much of the stress of arranging and paying for a funeral. In Spain and the Canary Islands, for instance, funerals usually take place within two or three days of death, which can make the release of funds to pay for it very difficult. A funeral plan helps to ease many of the problems that are often faced.

Meanwhile, get on with your life in the sun, but recognise that each day, as well as each gin and tonic, is a bonus. I promise that I will write something a little cheerier next time.

There's always a Funny Side to Life

The
Canary
Islander

Gorillas and Risk Assessments

A recent and very sad story about an uninformed vet working at a zoo in Tenerife set me thinking about risk assessments and contingency planning this week. Apparently, the poor vet accidentally shot a colleague, who was dressed as a gorilla, with a tranquilliser gun during an emergency training exercise. It was all part of contingency planning as to how staff should respond in an emergency situation involving these heavyweight animals. Protection of visitors, staff and the animals is, of course, very important for such establishments. Indeed, the very fact that the zoo had a training exercise in place at all impressed me.

I often think that the people of the Canary Islands have far more in common with Cuba or Venezuela than Peninsular Spain. Laid back attitudes to life, as well as the 'sloppy' version of the Castellano language, are more reminiscent of Latin America than the rather crisper approach to life demonstrated in Madrid. Risk assessment and contingency planning for something that may never happen is usually seen as unnecessary at best, and foolish at worst. I guess that this is one of the hardest things that I have had to come to terms with during my time living and working in Spain and the Canary Islands.

As a teacher, my life was always linked to 'what if?' scenarios. Ensuring the safety of children in our care was, quite rightly, of paramount importance. Plans and polices for health and safety, child protection, fire and civil emergencies, were all painfully written, discussed, checked, approved and regularly reviewed.

Contingency plans for staff absences, inclement weather, cycling safety, bus timetabling changes, quality of school meals (before the kitchens were closed), were often the stuff of staff and governors' meetings. As for preparing the curriculum and actually teaching the children, we usually managed to fit that in as well.

How different things are in Spain. When my partner and I launched, edited and ran a local newspaper on the island for a company in the Peninsular, I remember asking that, as we were a 'two-man band', what the plans were if one or both of us became ill or would like to take a holiday together. I remember the boss laughing and telling me that I was creating unnecessary problems. To me, it was little more than simple contingency planning, a sensible 'what if?' plan, in case the worst should happen. As it happened, the worst case scenario did happen and there was no contingency plan, but that is a story for another time.

The current popular situation with employment contracts in the Canary Islands, usually means that after eleven months of work, the employee is 'laid off' for a month and has to report to the unemployment office to claim benefit. The job that the employer used to fulfil is left vacant for a month and either colleagues are expected to work harder to fill the gap, or the job is not done until the absent colleague returns to work one month later. Unlike working in the UK, covering for absent colleagues simply does not happen over here.

There is precious little in the way of risk assessments and contingency planning that takes place in the

Canary Islands. Life is dealt with, or not dealt with, as it happens. If the postman takes a holiday, our letters are not delivered for a few weeks. If the owner of the village cafe bar's wife has a baby, the cafe bar remains closed for a few weeks. Should bank counter staff be ill, there is no one at the counter who is able to assist customers until they have recovered. After all, it does not lead to the end of the world, does it?

I have had to adjust my view of life to meet the situation that we are in now. However, I do applaud the good people operating the Tenerife zoo. In some ways, the freedom of not planning for 'what if' scenarios is refreshing and liberating. However, I often wish that a little more contingency planning would take place, just in case the worst should happen. Meanwhile, I can report that the man in the gorilla suit is recovering well and still talking to his colleague.

Nuts to Flying!

We all have those days when things seem to go wrong, without any reason at all. This was supposed to be a special day. It was the day when I was returning to the island of La Gomera, which is one of my favourite Canary Islands. It was going to be a particularly special break because, not only was it a short holiday, but also my birthday. I was also going to spend some time in one of the World's most spectacular heritage sites, the Garajonay National Park, which I had wanted to visit for some time.

Even though La Gomera is only a short distance away from my home on the neighbouring island of Gran Canaria, it did mean two short flights, courtesy of our local friendly airline. I was dreading the first part of the journey, because the flight into Tenerife to change planes is never a very pleasant experience; turbulence reigns with a vengeance, and is never comfortable in a small propeller type plane. Indeed, Tenerife seems to create more turbulence than most destinations that I have experienced.

As it was only a very short flight, there was hardly time for the customary inflight service. However, the all smiling, bountiful hostess leapt forward and suddenly presented me with what I thought was a bag of peanuts and a glass of sparkling water, which I thought was very brave considering how many bottles of sparkling water I have seen squirted over passengers in the past; sparkling drinks and aircraft do not mix. I accepted gratefully, and began to tuck into the peanuts. Those readers who know Spain well will know that the country's dentists are in league with the manufacturers of a particularly evil treat, that of 'frutos secos', which they say is a kind of dried fruit, but in reality comprises mainly of glass, lead and granite, spiced up with a little volcanic ash. The innocent looking packets do usually contain a few peanuts, which eases one into a false sense of security, and is something that I normally avoid.

We had not eaten since having an early breakfast and so I popped what I thought was a peanut into my mouth. Sadly, this was just as we were about to enter 'Tenerife airspace'. The place rocked and rolled, as it usually does when it hits heavy turbulence. The air hostess smiled benignly at some of her flight virgins, who looked extremely troubled as they were bumped and rocked around in the very small plane. We hit a particularly bad patch of turbulence just as I was enjoying what I thought was a peanut. It was not, and I felt something strange taking place in my mouth. As we bumped along, a little like one of the more significant rides at a theme park, a very large filling popped out of my mouth. My heart sank.

This was a particularly evil filling that I have had since my teenage years, so it has done rather well, but is not what I wanted on a Friday evening when staying on a small island in the Atlantic. As soon as we checked into the hotel, I made enquires about the whereabouts of a dental surgery. Needless to say, they were closed until Monday, but the very helpful receptionist did manage to call her friend, Carmen, who happened to be the receptionist of the only dentist on the island who was not on holiday, and made an appointment for my treatment first thing on Monday morning.

The following few days were interesting. Those readers who have lost a filling will know how the tongue tends to be drawn and catch on the offending tooth as if it were a magnet, causing damage to both tongue and eventually soreness in the throat. Within a day I could not speak, but eventually hit upon the idea of sticking a piece of chewing gum into the offending cavity. It helped, as did the copious glasses of whisky that my partner plied me with to ease my temper. Sadly, all the alcohol meant that I walked by mistake into a glass door of the hotel lobby and gave myself a black eye, which required a few stitches at the local hospital by a lovely young lady doctor. I hasten to add that I was not drunk, but merely tripped over an elderly, and none too pleased, chihuahua that was sunbathing by the front door. All the attention and kindness that I received almost made it worth the experience, but that is a story for another time.

Monday morning arrived. I don't think I have ever been quite so excited to see a dentist as I was on this occasion. Realising that there was only one dentist available on this small and remote island meant that I entered the surgery with some trepidation. I was concerned about how modern the equipment would be, and how it would compare with the space age surgery that I am used to at home. I needn't have worried. A brisk and efficient lady dentist appeared clutching a very large metal syringe. It was painless, although I was a little hurt that she seemed to think my experience with my tooth, as well as the black eye was amusing. My new filling was quickly in place, and I gratefully handed over the fee and fled to the nearest bar to recover from the experience.

The Case of the Exploding Shoes

Readers often write to tell me of the many and varied experiences that they face when beginning a new life in the sun. Often it is about their frustrations and misunderstandings with town halls, lawyers, as well as a lack of a decent Internet connection that prompts readers to write to me. However, a message from a reader living in the Costa Blanca a few weeks ago did intrigue me.

It was a message from a lady called Joan. One day, Joan decided to tidy the section of their wardrobe that belonged to her husband, Colin. He was a bit of a hoarder and had kept a pair of smart, expensive leather shoes that he had bought for work in the UK some ten years earlier. He thought that they might come in useful for weddings and funerals, but had never worn them since the couple left the UK. As he was out playing golf, Joan thought it was an ideal opportunity to lose them, and gain a little more space for herself.

As Joan picked up one of the shoes, the shoe exploded and spread a cloud of fine dust over her, the wardrobe and the bedroom. Needless to say, Joan was shocked; the same thing happened when she picked up the second shoe. It appears that the entire heel and sole of both shoes had completely disintegrated with age and the heat.

Joan's email reminded me of a warning that I gave a few weeks ago about the deterioration of rubber in car tyres, and was the reason why tyres should be changed every six years, regardless of the amount of tread remaining. The sun and heat causes rubber related products to deteriorate very quickly, and in the case of tyres, become very dangerous. I replied briefly to Joan, and gave the issue no more thought until this week.

A few days ago, I discovered a pair of trainers that I had bought some time ago in a sale. They were a highly reputable, and usually expensive, brand, which had been for sale at a price that I could not resist. I remember immediately regretting buying them when I got home, as there were a little too tight for me, and so they had remained in a wardrobe in the vague hope that they may fit when the weather became cooler.

As we had a cool spell, I decided that now was the time, and I put the trainers on to take Bella, our dog, for a walk. I managed to walk just a hundred metres from our home, when there was strange squelching sound, and I found myself sinking gently to the ground. Bella fled down the path with both horror and embarrassment. Yes, you guessed; one of my trainers had exploded, leaving a cloud of fine white granules spread all over the road. It was a weird and unsettling experience, and as I turned to return home before anyone witnessed my predicament, the second trainer burst, leaving another cloud of dust and the bottom of the shoe on the road.

It was as I was hopping home that a neighbour caught me. Don't these meetings always happen at a bad time? After initial greetings, he commented that I look troubled, and was everything OK? Had I hurt myself, he asked kindly, as he had noticed that I had developed a rather serious limp. I thanked him, and did my best to muster up as much dignity as possible as I struggled down the road to our gate, with only the top of the trainers covering my feet.

If you are reading this, Joan, I empathise and urge all readers living in the sun to check the contents of their wardrobes, and to carefully check the age and condition of their shoes.

It's a Brit Thing

All nationalities have their own funny little ways of doing things, and the British are no exception to the rule. Indeed, I sometimes think that, as a nation, we tend to go out of our way to be awkward and to do things rather differently from the rest of Continental Europe. This is not deliberate of course, it just happens that way. Let me give you a few examples.

I will never get used to continental electricity plugs, sockets and light fittings. They look positively dangerous to me. I am used to those good, solid three pin plugs with a green earth wire for good measure. That green wire is just so reassuring. Used throughout the UK and Ireland, they look and feel much safer that the flimsy two pin efforts that are used in Europe. Mind you, even they are sublime design creations when compared to the flimsy prongs to be found on electric plugs in the US and Canada. Where did they get that idea?

As for light fittings, just don't get me started on that one. I managed to electrocute myself a few weeks ago whilst changing a light bulb in our bathroom. I have never previously switched off electricity at the mains before just changing a light bulb, but apparently I should have done. Silly me, I thought that when the light switch was 'off' no electricity was coming through the circuit. Apparently this is not the case over here, and I am fortunate that I was only standing on a low pair of steps at the time, and did not have my hands in water. Anyway, it did give the electrician a few laughs when he checked out our circuitry. Not only is our system in perfect condition, but I was then lectured about how I should always switch off at the mains first... I felt like a five-year-old.

Those readers who have visited Spain and the Canary Islands will also know that kettles are never provided in hotel bedrooms. This is, of course, to ensure that visitors only purchase drinks from the hotel bar. However, for those of you who go self-catering on holiday, have you noticed that only very rarely is a kettle provided? Usually, it is one of those rather silly saucepans with two handles. Whoever heard of boiling water for a cup of tea in a two-handled saucepan? Most sensible travellers that I know always carry a portable kettle in their suitcase, just in case.

Bread makers and slow cookers? Well, until recently you could forget trying to get those two wonderful appliances in Spain and the Canary Islands. I know of many who have brought their bread makers with them from the UK, and were unable to replace them when they finally died. As for slow cookers, well I was told by one lady in a department store that as Canarians never did anything slowly there would be no market for them. I am still trying to work that one out.

Did I mention two-handled saucepans? Yes, I resolutely refuse to call them pans, but will stick to the term that I have grown up with - saucepans. As a Brit, I really do detest those two handled things, particularly as most do not have insulated handles and so even the most dedicated of chefs needs asbestos hands to handle them. I recently had to search most of the Canary Islands to find a decent set of saucepans with one handle, but in the end I had to order a set from Amazon. Thank goodness for Jamie Oliver!

I rather like the single-handled variety of saucepan, because I can hold the saucepan with one hand and stir or read with the other. I am no chef, but it seems logical enough to me. I suspect that the two-handled variety to be a cunning invention of the French to throw the Brits off guard. Of course, the chefs over here tell me that the two-handled varieties of pan are perfect for putting in the oven. Come off it, who in real life actually puts a saucepan in the oven anyway? Mind you, it's not all bad; I really do like our magnificent Spanish paella pan.

A Nice Cup of Tea

As all true Brits know, it is impossible to get a decent cup of tea abroad. Many have tried over the years, and failed miserably. Tea is the true Brit's favourite beverage, closely followed by a large gin and tonic, and is one of the reasons that life abroad fails miserably for some.

No one but a true Brit really understands all the fuss over a "Nice Cup of Tea": It is the stuff that unites as well as steadies the nerves of the nation and, according, to Winston Churchill, wins wars against all the odds. When fate decides to deal one of its more cruel blows, the true Brit rushes for the teapot, sits down and reflects over a "Nice Cup of Tea". Indeed, it is often said that tea is the stuff that runs through the veins of the true Brit.

Wise Brits on holiday always travel with a kettle, albeit of the small suitcase variety. Many even travel with their own packets of tea, because they are convinced that the stuff for sale in continental supermarkets isn't the real thing, but a rather nasty 'look a like' variety designed to appease the discerning British holidaymaker. Asking for a cup of tea in most bars or hotels, usually guarantees a shrug followed by the arrival of a nasty stainless steel teapot filled with luke warm water, together with a fusty teabag containing mouse droppings. Sadly, even one's own kettle and a supply of tea, albeit as teabags, produces a really nasty cup of tea in the hotel bedroom. This really is the stuff to make the discerning British tea drinker pack up and go home, determined to holiday in Brighton the following year.

So, what about the British resident? How do they survive? Well, not very well, by all accounts. I firmly believe that this is the reason why so many people wear a scowl rather than a smile in the sunshine. Of course, if asked, they blame the European Union for not being able to get a "Nice Cup of Tea", but then again, they blame the EU for most things anyway. Until recently, some of our friends always asked us to bring packets of Yorkshire Tea back for them whenever we visited the UK. Despite considerable efforts over several years, including the installation of an expensive water filtration and water softening system, they could cope no longer and finally fled back to the UK, teapot in hand, to resume their lives and to delight once again in enjoying "A Nice Cup of Tea".

Of course, the real problem is the water. Foreign water just isn't like the 'real' water from Britain. After all, it has been pumped with chemicals, often desalinated and usually unfit to drink, isn't it? Sadly, most are blind to all the impurities in the water that they drink in the UK, and remain obstinate to the facts that water standards in mainland Europe are often much higher than in the UK. How about bottled water? That is the same stuff poured into bottles and sold at a ridiculously high price, isn't it? Most people take the view that whilst expensive bottled French water with a posh name maybe all right to swill your dentures in at night, it is certainly not the stuff to pour over a precious teabag.

The true Brit quickly accepts the fact that "A Nice Cup of Tea" is impossible to find once one passes the

White Cliffs of Dover. It is best to accept one's fate and realise that a lifetime of drinking decent coffee in continental bars and restaurants looms, and is far preferable to drinking an overpriced soup bowl of the foul stuff served in most of the new chains of coffee bars that seem to have sprung up overnight across the UK.

Everyone develops their own coping strategies. Personally, I still get pangs for a "Nice Cup of Tea" at around 4.00pm each afternoon. I have partly resolved the issue by now only drinking green tea, with no milk or sugar, which I agree is an acquired taste. I prefer to use a china teapot, cup and saucer, never a mug, and if served with a nice fresh scone and jam, so much the better. Being a Brit in all this sunshine really isn't easy, but I am getting used to it.

Mutiny on the Ferry

Well, we all know what it is like. You've had a busy day being a very important captain of a not too important ship. You've had an early start and only eaten a dry cheese and pickle sandwich for lunch. You are hot and tired, and you can feel a headache coming on. What's more, you just can't wait to get home to the dog, or the wife... How about skipping part of the journey and hopping along to another destination port instead? That would be a very sensible idea, which would make life so much easier. You would arrive home much earlier and maybe the passengers, who are so tanked up with cheap booze anyway, won't even notice. After all, this is the Canary Islands, and it would be hard to be more chilled out. Maybe, but possibly think again.

The island ferry was on one of its regular sailings from the island of Fuerteventura to Las Palmas on the island of Gran Canaria. The service is never particularly exciting; it is just one of the many standard ferry journeys to facilitate the connections between the seven Canary Islands. The ferry had already been delayed for some time, and the passengers were not pleased at its late departure from Fuerteventura and its even later arrival in Gran Canaria. The last straw came when an announcement over the ferry's public address system indicated that the ferry would dock at the port of Agaete instead, and not Las Palmas as timetabled, making it a much longer journey, which would mean further delays and inconvenience for the passengers on board. Do passengers matter that much anyway? The captain made a decision; he would not stop at the planned destination, but travel on to Agaete. Wouldn't the company be pleased with him?

The passengers were not happy when they heard the news. Indeed, it quickly became clear that they were having none of it and, after a brief meeting, angrily decided that they would stage a protest and insist that the ship's captain think again and stick to the original destination. Seeing the numbers of angry passengers on board, the captain, wisely, reconsidered his earlier decision and decided to head for the port of Las Palmas as originally scheduled. A wise man indeed.

Apparently, the planned switch to Agaete had nothing to do with poor weather conditions or safety issues, but was merely to address the issue that one of the company's other ferries was not in service, and it suited the interests and economics of the company to use the Fuerteventura ferry to fulfil its scheduled service to Tenerife. The passengers won the day and disembarked in Las Palmas as originally planned. Victory for the travellers and common sense prevailed.

So there we have it. The captain, as well as the shipping company learned a valuable lesson, and, for once, passengers reigned supreme. If you just happen to be a captain of a ship, a bus driver or a pilot, never be tempted to switch to another route just because you happen to have changed your mind or you need to be at a party. It is best to stick to the original route, otherwise you may have a mutiny on board.

Printed in Dunstable, United Kingdom